The Heart of Community

The Heart of Community

A Family Journey

George Rupp

WIPF & STOCK · Eugene, Oregon

THE HEART OF COMMUNITY
A Family Journey

Wipf & Stock
An Imprint of Wipf and Stock Publishers
199 W. 8th Ave., Suite 3
Eugene, OR 97401

www.wipfandstock.com

PAPERBACK ISBN: 978-1-7252-8439-5
HARDCOVER ISBN: 978-1-7252-8440-1
EBOOK ISBN: 978-1-7252-8441-8

Manufactured in the U.S.A.   08/12/20

Contents

Acknowledgments

I WOULD LIKE TO express my appreciation for the work of the Wipf & Stock team in the publication of this book. I am especially grateful to K. C. Hanson—and also to Michael West, my friend and colleague from Harvard Divinity School, for introducing us to each other. K. C. has invested impressive attention and energy in executing tasks that he as editor in chief could easily have delegated to others. I am pleased to register my heartfelt thanks. I appreciate as well members of the staff at Wipf and Stock, in particular Rachel Saunders and George Callihan, for excellent support at each step of the way. To all of you, thank you very much.

Photos

Preface

MUCH OF MY WRITING over the years has been concerned with the theme of individualism and the quest for community. In this memoir, I have focused on a personal family narrative and have deliberately resisted the temptation to indulge in the often quite abstract issues that I address in my previous books. But in this preface, I will take the liberty of connecting the two patterns even as I invite readers who are impatient for the more personal narrative to skip the next three paragraphs.

Here then is a very brief overview of how this memoir is related to my previous works. My first book—*Christologies and Cultures: Toward a Typology of Religious Worldviews*—builds on the Western medieval debate between Nominalism and Realism to develop an axis of differentiation among worldviews in terms of whether the individual or the universal is of primary significance. Similarly, my *Beyond Existentialism and Zen: Religion in a Pluralistic World* argues for the imperative to move beyond both the individualism that Western existentialism illustrates and the undifferentiated universalism that the Zen version of Buddhist tradition may be taken to typify.

The following four books then illustrate my efforts to develop an inclusive sense of community that includes self-critical and comparative dimensions. *Culture-Protestantism: German Liberal Theology at the Turn of the Twentieth Century* pursues that goal through an examination of the thought of Ernst Troeltsch in the context of the multiple strains of German liberal theology and its critics (notably Karl Barth). *Commitment and Community* in turn argues for the commitment to particular communities that at the same time engage constructively with the broader society. The next two books continue this exploration, as the titles illustrate. *Globalization Challenged: Conviction, Conflict, Community* draws in particular on my experience with the International Rescue Committee to register the crucial roles of conviction and community in both the generation and the resolution of conflicts. Similarly, *Beyond Individualism: The Challenge of Inclusive Communities* extends the argument more broadly to both educational and activist engagement. In sum, the six books pursue a shared agenda of advocating for communities based on particular commitments that aspire to become increasingly inclusive even while retaining their allegiance to the individuals at their core.

While family is not a prominent motif in these books, it appears remarkably consistently in the dedication of each volume (here listed in the order in which the six books were written): For Nancy [my wife]; For Kathy and Stephanie [our daughters]; For my parents, Erika Braunöhler Rupp and Gustav Wilhelm Rupp; For Erika, Nancy, Kathy, and Stephanie; For Alex, Leo, Kai-Lin, Erika, and Kai-Shan [five of our six grandchildren, the sixth of whom, Kai-Jin, was born just after the book was published]; For Nancy—my closest companion for fifty-five years.

This memoir is intended to complement those previous books by offering a personal narrative of the family journey at the heart of my reflections on particular and inclusive communities. The order of the narrative is straightforwardly chronological. It therefore begins with Nancy's and my early lives and then includes our daughters as they were growing up with us and, more synoptically, as they pursued higher education and work, married, and had children of their own.

The result is a narrative divided into four parts—call them quarters, each plus or minus twenty years: 1942–1964; 1964–1985; 1985–2002; 2002–.

First Quarter

From Henniker and Springfield

(1942–1964)

NANCY HAD THE MORE varied early years. She was born in University Hospital of Ohio State University in Columbus, Ohio, the first child in her family. Her parents, Prescott Farrar (known as Pres) and Katherine Hitchcock Farrar (usually called Polly) were deeply-rooted New Englanders, who lived in Columbus while her father completed a master's degree in dairy technology.

She then moved with her parents to New Hampshire to the Farrar family farm, where her father helped her grandfather with milk production as part of the effort to maintain food levels during World War II. She has fond memories of life on the farm with her parents and grandparents—in particular of adventures with her father, who let her ride on work horses and go with him on hunting trips. (After Nancy and I were dating, allocating time for at least a brief stay at the annual family camp on the grounds of original 1700s Farrar land, now woods, between Henniker and Hillsboro that the family called "the back place" was required and enjoyed.)

But by the time Nancy entered school, the family had moved to a house in the town center, which proudly declared itself "the only Henniker on earth." Here she continued to be very close to her best childhood friend, Carolyn Fitch (now Patenaude), with whom she has remained in steady touch over the seven intervening decades. Nancy and her family then moved again when she was ten to the suburbs of Philadelphia, where her father had taken a new job with a dairy equipment production company after his years as a dairy farmer and then a state milk inspector in New Hampshire.

At least in terms of locations, I had the less varied childhood. I was born in Overlook Hospital in Summit, New Jersey, and lived in Springfield, NJ (next-door town) and Mountainside, NJ (also a next-door town) for the next seventeen years. In contrast to Nancy's parents, who traced their American lineage back to the Mayflower on both sides of the family, my parents were German immigrants: my father, known to me as "Pop" but named Gustav, in 1930 from the Black Forest region of Germany; and my mother, Erika Braunöhler, in 1937 from the Rheinland. So my family came from great distances but stayed in the same small area of New Jersey for many years.

Yet despite my living steadily in New Jersey for my first seventeen years, I was unusual at my birth in that I was completely unexpected. Mom was a twin, and she was pretty sure that the size of her womb indicated she was carrying twins. But her doctor (also an immigrant, though in his case from Cuba) assured her that there was only one heartbeat. So I had to raise my hand or otherwise assert myself after my brother Herb was born to be sure I would be allowed into the world three minutes later.

After that dramatic entry, as youngsters within two years of each other in age, my brothers and I played in the tree nursery behind our house at 89 Colfax Road in Springfield and then relished such activities as working with friends to build a small village of underground rooms and later also above-ground huts in the woods after the nursery was sold for development and in effect more or less offered lumber for off-site construction.

With my brothers, I also worked for pay from age nine on. When brother Pete turned eleven (the threshold age for becoming a newspaper deliverer), he acquired a triple-sized newspaper route and allowed brother Herb and me each to take on a third of it and to deliver papers by bike to about a hundred homes every day. Within a few years, the three of us then also became the core team that compiled the many sections of many hundreds of newspapers (some ten brands in all, including the *New York Times*) on Sundays (starting at 3:30 a.m.) for distribution to an entire network of deliverers across a handful of towns around our hometown of Springfield.

By our early teens we also developed a business in cutting lawns, in particular in the upscale next-door town of Short Hills. Pete even printed up calling cards for the Rupp Brothers as "experienced lawn cutters," which we used to offer services by leaving them on the doors of prospective further clients. (Pete printed the cards on his own retrieved and rebuilt printing press at about age twelve.)

I will not indulge in details about all of the other jobs I held as a teenager, but I cannot resist mentioning two. One was in the local Grand Union store, in which I became employed at age sixteen as a member of the Retail Workers Union. I worked there through my remaining years of high school, and I did every job from mopping floors to restocking shelves to working the checkout register. The second was my employment in construction: I became quite experienced in building the wood frames that are the core of conventional American housing—a skill I exercised in summers during the latter part of high schools and some of the summers during college as well.

My parents kept in close touch with other immigrants from Germany through the German Y (CVJM—German initials for Christian Association of Young Men), which met regularly at the McBurney Y on 23rd Street between 7th and 8th Avenues in Manhattan (it later moved to 14th Street). My memories are still vivid of driving over the Pulaski Skyway and through the Holland Tunnel to attend celebrative gatherings at least every Christmas and Easter and in most years several more times as well. There were as well visits among the families at their homes on all sides of the Manhattan where they had met and also at a camp on Bear Mountain where they regularly gathered at a camp of log houses.

My family stayed in even closer touch with the only relatives of my parents' generation in this country: the Braunöhlers—the family of my mother's brother Otto, who had married Hilda Heitmann, whose parents were both German immigrants, though she herself was born in the United States. The three Braunohler (Uncle Otto decided to drop the umlaut on the "o" soon after he arrived to make the name easier for Americans to pronounce) children were the only cousins that my brothers and I had in this country, and we were very close, living about half an hour apart in New Jersey and getting together at least a handful of times every year. Of the six cousins, Ingrid was the oldest by a year or two, Walter was next (a year older than Pete), and Bob was the youngest (a few years younger than Herb and I).

Of a great many adventures, perhaps the most memorable is building a vacation home in Eliot, Maine, on the Piscataqua River while the senior Rupps were on a business trip to California. The foreman was Unk (as in Uncle Otto), and the crew was the boy cousins, who at that time ranged in age from about eight to about fifteen. (Ingrid was also there, but she was more interested in her boyfriend Clyde, who was from that very area and would be her husband by the time they were both college juniors.) In two weeks of very hard work, the house was framed and enclosed, with only interior work left to do the next year.

Nancy and I first met at the Jonathan Dayton Regional High School, where we were both members of what was to be the Class of 1960. I was still living in Springfield, where our high school was located. Nancy had moved with her family (now five children of whom she was the oldest) to 796 Mountain Avenue in Berkeley Heights, which was then one of the five towns that had Jonathan Dayton Regional as their high school. (It might be worth noting that along with Mountainside it was at the high end of the socioeconomic and intellectual spectrum—in part because Bell Laboratories had its research facility in neighboring Murray Hill—with the towns of Kenilworth and Garwood at the other end of the spectrum as almost exclusively blue collar working class places and Springfield in the middle.)

Nancy and I did not become more than slightly acquainted in the first two years of high school. In retrospect, it may be because Nancy was at the forefront of the physical development of her classmates, while I was a late bloomer. Wrestling was the right sport for me because I was small and slight but had always had to be tough and scrappy to keep from being bullied. So wrestling at 105 pounds in freshman year was just right—even if I then weighed less than 100 pounds.

For her part, Nancy related to the intellectual leaders among our classmates and members of the next few older classes, those who dominated the debate team and took courses like Foundations of Western Civilization, while I focused on math and science courses, in part because I could do them without much time or effort and thereby allow time for work at the local Grand Union grocery store. (It may be worth noting that one of the rules I observed all through high school was not ever to take a book home for homework.)

The Rupp family moved from Springfield to Mountainside after my freshman year—to a house that realized my father's dream of having a wonderful view, in this case from the first range of hills in from the coast out to the Manhattan in which he had first lived and worked after arriving in the U.S. I also began my multiple years of building houses by working on a small crew led by the brothers who constructed the Mountainside home as they then continued to build in surrounding communities in subsequent years.

After the move, my family continued to attend the First Presbyterian Church in Springfield. Pop served on the session, and Mom was also active in church programs. There was a large and growing youth group at the church, led by a charismatic young assistant minister named George Forner, in which Pete, Herb, and I all participated. I became the president of the group, which grew to over 100 high school age kids. Connections to this church remained strong: Nancy and I were married there; both Kathy and Stephie were baptized there; I was ordained to the Presbyterian ministry there; and my parents are buried in the church cemetery.

Nancy's family was also active in Berkeley Heights. After initially attending a Presbyterian Church in nearby Summit, Nancy's father was centrally involved in the group that established a satellite church in Berkeley Heights—about a block from the Farrar home. (Nancy and I still have a large oak coffee table that is used every day, which her father made out of a huge slice of a tree that he cut down on the property where the church was constructed.) Nancy's father was also engaged in Berkeley Heights governance, serving as a member of the Planning Commission, the local planning and zoning board. All five of the Farrar siblings participated in a wide range of social and athletic activities from the time they moved to Berkeley Heights, as they had been during their years in Pennsylvania.

By junior year, Nancy and I began dating. Each of us continued to have other dating interests—perhaps Nancy more than I. But by spring of our junior year, we were pretty steady partners, including the junior prom. As junior year moved into senior year, we began to coordinate our post-high school plans. Nancy was quite clear in her own mind that she needed to minimize the costs of her higher education because her parents still had her four siblings to support through their educations. I had grades and test scores that would probably allow me to go wherever I would have liked. Since neither of my parents had attended universities, the family agreed that Princeton as the best local university would be a fine choice. Nancy looked at Douglas (the then women's part of what is now co-educational Rutgers University) but decided that she didn't care for the students she met there. So in pretty short order, the decision was Trenton State College, now the College of New Jersey, for Nancy and Princeton for me.

At Trenton State, Nancy pursued her goal of becoming a junior and senior high school teacher, and I followed a general course of study that would keep options open. I thought of majoring in math, but my first-year honors calculus course convinced me that the subject was too abstract and theoretical to be of long-term interest—unlike theology or comparative religion! (This calculus course started with a proof that the number one existed and then proceeded to "prove" every step from there forward. On the day I decided that I would not major in math, the professor had been working on a proof for two periods and had proceeded around three of the four blackboards on the walls of the room. Suddenly he stepped back from the board and said, "What's going on here?" His proof was not jelling in the sense that the last step didn't yield 1=1 but rather +1 = -1! Of the twenty-five students in the room, not one had followed the steps of the proof closely enough to be able to help in finding the error!) In any case, I did not major in math, and I also did not take a single religion course, since I felt that if I went to seminary after college, that would allow plenty of time to study whatever there was to learn about religion. On the side, I continued with other activities: working (notably getting up at 5 a.m. to drive the truck that delivered newspapers to campus locations for others to deliver them to rooms in the dorms), rowing crew, and organizing a team of students to tutor kids at the Jamesburg Reformatory each week. Nancy and I also managed to get together virtually every week, facilitated by the car that I had purchased and that was kept on the Trenton State campus. Along with quality time with each other, we also participated in the Presbyterian student youth group on the Princeton campus and attended the predominantly African American Witherspoon Presbyterian Church in Princeton.

Happily, both Nancy and I were able to arrange to spend our junior year of college (1962–63) in Europe—Nancy as an exchange student in Dundee, Scotland, and I in Munich, Germany, as a student in the junior year abroad program of Wayne State University. This program was administered from Detroit, Michigan, but admitted students from across the country, which was great, since Princeton did not at the time have any of its own opportunities for study abroad.

For me the year in Germany was an extraordinary opportunity to become acquainted with those of my closest relatives who had not emigrated to the United States, most of whom I had not met before. The exceptions were my mother's twin sister Ruth and their mother, my grandmother, both of whom had visited us in

New Jersey. During this year abroad I then also had the chance to meet my other aunts and uncles and cousins. It was a wonderful experience. In effect, I met two halves of my personality embodied in very different families in two distinctive parts of Germany—Baden Württemberg and the Rheinland.

As for our studies, Nancy continued her teacher education, including student teaching in local Scottish schools. During her studies, teaching, and dormitory living, she met fellow students and their families, with whom she kept in touch for many decades. I had a mechanical engineering student as my roommate, and I studied German philosophy and literature. I also took two semesters of accelerated Greek, designed for German students who had neglected to learn Greek in high school, for which I kept a four-column vocabulary book—Greek, Latin (in which the rendering was first given for the German students who had studied Latin in high school), German, and English. Nancy was assured credit for her junior year because she was an official exchange student. I, too, was assured credit (at zero tuition more or less by default, since virtually no one studied abroad then), although I had to write my junior papers and complete my junior-year general exams, which were mailed to a faculty member who agreed to supervise the time for the six-hour exam and then return the text to Princeton for grading.

Perhaps the most rewarding and certainly the most enjoyable time during this year was traveling all over western Europe—mostly in the 1949 Volkswagen that I purchased for $125 when I arrived in Europe. Nancy and I would meet whenever we could and certainly for every vacation. In the course of the year, in addition to England and Scotland and Germany, we traveled to or at least through Austria, Italy, Switzerland, France, Denmark, Sweden, Holland, Belgium, and Luxembourg. It was eye-opening at a time when there were not yet so many American tourists in Europe. It also had the unexpected result of making us acutely aware that, however critical we may have been of the United States (I in particular), we were also pretty deeply convinced Americans.

Junior year ended by early summer. In the course of that year, Nancy and I decided to get married after graduation from college and therefore returned to the U.S. to earn money and get ready for senior year and the wedding to follow. I went back to employment on a house construction crew, allowing time to work as a community organizer for a few weeks with St. John's Church, a predominantly African-American church in Jersey City. Nancy returned to multiple jobs and family responsibilities. Late that summer of 1963 Nancy and I also became formally engaged with the plan to marry the following summer.

In the intervening months, we completed our studies (including a senior thesis for me) and graduated from college, Nancy as a certified English teacher and I with a little known comparative literature major in the English department. Nancy received accolades, including graduating with honors and election to Kappa Delta Pi (the national honor society for education); and I graduated with high honors, a Phi Beta Kappa key, and perhaps most important for the future, a multi-year Danforth Foundation Fellowship for graduate study. My work that summer back at St. John's Church in Jersey City included participation in a demonstration to protest the abysmal condition of low-income housing that the city managed. The demonstration led to my arrest and jailing—though I was released in time (with several days to spare) for the wedding on August 22, 1964, which rounds out the first quarter of this overview.

Second Quarter

To Cambridge Five Times

(1964–1985)

THE SECOND QUARTER BEGINS with a wonderful honeymoon on a tiny island in the middle of a small lake in northern New York, a camping trip across Canada, and then a meeting of the Society for Values in Higher Education, a sort of alumni/ae group of the recipients of Danforth Graduate Fellowships. After dropping off Nancy's brother Charlie at a camp en route to our honeymoon island, she and I enjoyed time alone together until we got to the Danforth meeting in Michigan for a stimulating conference— though neither of us remembers much of it.

After the honeymoon, we drove to New Haven, where I was going to begin my studies for a BD (Bachelor of Divinity!) at Yale Divinity School, and Nancy was starting a master's program in English at Southern Connecticut State University—both supported through the Danforth Foundation grant, which not only provided a generous stipend to cover living expenses but also paid tuition for both the awardee and his or her spouse.

At Yale Divinity School, I continued my engagement in activist causes. As a member of CORE (the Congress on Racial Equality) from my Jersey City involvements, I decided to attend CORE meetings in New Haven and as a result had a vivid sense of racial tensions there. I also became involved very quickly in anti-Vietnam war activities—truth be told, before they were known as such. I was among the first members of Americans for the Reappraisal of Far Eastern Policy (ARFEP)—a gathering of individuals whom Bill Coffin and Staughton Lynd convened to oppose what was to become the war in Vietnam, though no one yet referred to it that way. I also continued to be active in civil rights agitation in New Haven and, for example, in participating in a delegation of five (which included Nancy) to McComb, Mississippi, in response to a call from the National Council of Churches for witnesses to come to help prevent further church bombings.

In my second year, I became the chair of the Social Action Committee of the YDS Association (whose membership remarkably included faculty and staff as well as students). In this capacity I pressed for active engagement on both civil rights and anti-war causes. At YDS, many in positions of authority considered me to be an extremist. But it was a time of considerable turmoil in opinions. In the spring of 1966, for example, my good friend Bud Ogle and I debated a faculty member in social ethics, David Little, and his teaching assistant, John Reeder, on ethical issues raised by the war in Vietnam to an overflowing crowd. It was therefore a stunning moment for the school when I was elected as president of the YDS Association—at a time when sources in the dean's office disclosed internal messages that expressed concern about the communists who were taking over the school.

I also worked away at my studies and in a series of field work placements as well. During the three academic years, that field work was at the Yale Psychiatric Institute, at a predominantly African-American Church in the Dixwell neighborhood of New Haven, and at Cheshire Academy, where I taught religion. In addition, Nancy and I spent one summer as teachers of incoming students at Tennessee A & I University in Nashville and a second summer in Waverly, Ohio, as community workers in rural Appalachian villages. As for my studies, my time at YDS allowed me to catch up on all of those courses that I had not taken as an undergraduate, including biblical studies, the history of Christianity and of Western philosophy, systematic theology, and sociology of religion.

During these years Nancy was also very busy. She completed her course work for her master's degree at Southern Connecticut State University in one year and then proceeded to teach eighth grade at the junior high school in near-by Branford for the next two years. She would complete the requirements for the degree a few years later with her thesis on George Elliot. Nancy also managed a small household very effectively and with regrettably little help from me. Both Nancy and I enjoyed getting to know the fellow students and spouses who lived in the same building, some of whom have remained life-long friends.

Nancy and I had decided not to have children in these first years of our marriage. But by year three, we decided it was time to begin the process of building a family. I was admitted for doctoral study at Yale, but I chose not to stay because I was frustrated with the overwhelming mood of Neo-Orthodoxy in general and admiration of Karl Barth in particular. Instead, I was drawn to Harvard because there I could better combine my interest in Christian theology and the comparative study of religion. Nancy was open to a move, especially since she was also happy about starting a family, which might in any case interrupt her teaching career. Still, to cover all contingencies, in advance of the move she secured a teaching position in the town of Harvard, Massachusetts.

Nancy and I then prepared for the move from New Haven to Cambridge, where we had been offered and accepted an apartment at the Center for the Study of World Religions. As the move commenced (via U-Haul truck and family car), Nancy found that she was pregnant. We moved into our apartment. Nancy felt it was best to inform her new school that she was pregnant while there was still time to recruit a replacement so that the year would not be interrupted for the students. After the school did indeed find a replacement, Nancy was about to be a stay-at-home expectant mother when neighbors at the Center informed her and me that they, too, had a change in their plans. They had intended to be house parents at a women's dormitory at Pine Manor Junior College in Chestnut Hill, Massachusetts, but now could not accept that appointment because of other commitments. They asked whether, in view of Nancy's changed circumstances, she and I might have interest in this opportunity. After interviews and the usual formalities, Nancy was selected as the resident counselor of Southwest, a small residence hall on the edge of the campus. As the dormitory mother, Nancy was allowed to bring me along as the dormitory father, and the two of us moved in by the end of the summer. Six months later, Katherine Heather was born on February 14, Valentine's Day, 1968, and began her life in Southwest with thirty-eight older "sisters"— only a little younger than her own parents.

Nancy, Kathy, and I lived in the resident counselor's apartment. Nancy worked with students and staff colleagues, while I commuted to Cambridge for classes and other duties, which included work as a teaching assistant in several courses over two years. I then took my PhD general exams at the end of my second year in the program. During that second year, I also made plans, with Nancy's concurrence, to spend a third year (1969–70) in Sri Lanka (then still called Ceylon) to study Theravada Buddhism. I certainly knew that I would never have the languages and other knowledge to be an expert in Buddhism, but I was very interested in serious exposure to a tradition in addition to Western Christianity.

I passed my general exams and then, with support from Harvard's Center for the Study of World Religions (which included round-the world flight tickets with unlimited stops en route), Nancy and I and baby Kathy set off for Ceylon. On the way to Ceylon, we made time to see friends and to see new sights in England, Scotland, Germany, Greece, and India, and then on the way back, stops included India, Myanmar (then Burma), Thailand, Hong Kong, Japan, Hawaii, Arizona (where my brother Herb was studying for an MBA at the Thunderbird School), and Louisiana (where my brother Pete and his new wife Marie were then living).

It was a remarkable year! I learned a lot about Buddhism, including what I valued and what I did not value so much in the multiple traditions within Buddhism. I also confirmed Nancy's and my sense that my impatience rendered me a tough candidate for meditation, even when taught by the leading meditation instructor in Ceylon, who also happened to be a Jewish refugee from Nazi Germany who enjoyed discussing Spinoza in German with me after my meditation efforts. Nancy completed her master's thesis on influences of Ludwig Feuerbach on George Elliot and met friends with whom she kept in touch for decades. At the same time, Kathy had a stimulating second year of life. It included seeing much that she thinks she remembers, though most of those memories are probably more of photos than of the events themselves—including her first exposure to Japan as a passenger on our back-pack carrier, which fascinated Japanese observers because such contraptions were not then used in Japan.

On returning from the adventurous year in Asia, our family again lived at Pine Manor Junior College, where Nancy was now the resident counselor for a much larger complex of residence halls—some one hundred fifty students. Both Nancy and I enjoyed interactions with these students, even including dividing up the waiting for the return of students who had signed out for the evening. I worked both in the Pine Manor library and in a cubicle in the Divinity School library in Cambridge on my dissertation, which developed a typology of religious worldviews generated from different Christian interpretations of the significance of Christ and then compared those positions to the diversity of Buddhist traditions. I also served as a teaching assistant for Harvard Divinity School courses. Specifically, I worked with Dick (Richard R.) Niebuhr and also audited a course on Hegel's *Logic* that I had persuaded Gordon Kaufman to offer. So I was fortunate to be in very close touch with my two closest teachers and advisors as I wrote my dissertation.

Nancy and I were also looking into next steps in continuing to grow our family and in future career choices after the completion of both of our programs of graduate study. The outcome of the first of those prospects was eagerly anticipated from the fall on and was settled on May 3, 1971, with the birth of Stephanie Karin (three days after the medical expenses were covered by the university health insurance that had been discontinued during the year abroad). The second outcome was clear at the same time as I considered options for work after completing my PhD. Remarkably, in view of the very tight job market for PhDs, I had four choices. In the end, the one I elected was the riskiest—an experimental college in Redlands, California: Johnston College, which had no general graduation requirements (but rather individualized graduation contracts), no grades (but rather written evaluations), no departments (so as to encourage interdisciplinary study) and no tenure for faculty (but rather renewable contracts).

In Redlands, Nancy and Kathy and Stephanie/Stephie and I wound up living in our first house: 815 Monterrey St. It was a small (1300 square feet) three-bedroom house with a lovely enclosed back yard that allowed, in addition to a living room and dining room and bedroom for Nancy and me, a small bright bedroom for Kathy and Stephie, a study (mostly for me), and a play room surrounded with views to the back yard. Nancy served as vice president of a parent-run child care center connected with the university that offered pre-school programs, which both Kathy and Stephie attended. After a year, Kathy then also enjoyed attending the local school, which was within walking distance. During those years, our family attended the Impact Presbyterian Church, a wonderfully inclusive community across a range of ethnic identities.

I taught classes (all discussion-based and often co-taught with colleagues—as in one called "Space and Time," with professors of biology, physics, philosophy, and me as the teachers). I also attended endless community meetings as part of the shared governance of Johnston College. Then, at the end of second year, I was asked to serve as Vice Chancellor—even though I was then the youngest member of the faculty. I loved all of my time at Johnston, including my first experience in administration. I also had the pleasure of seeing a book version of my dissertation published as *Christologies and Cultures: Toward a Typology of Religious Worldviews.* But in the fall of our third year in Redlands, just as I was settling in to my double role as Faculty Fellow in Religion and Vice Chancellor, Harvard Divinity School approached me about whether I would be willing to return to Cambridge to be a fill-in for one of my mentors, Dick Niebuhr, who was taking a leave to launch a (much-belated) undergraduate program in religion in Harvard College. After conflicted deliberation, Nancy and I decided that the answer was yes.

After the decision was made but before the move, my father died. He had had a serious heart condition since his early forties, probably stemming from the rheumatic fever he had as a child. He was for decades limited in how much physical labor he could do—which is why my brothers and I did all of the heavy work in the yard while we were still home. But his death was sudden and unexpected: he simply fell over dead after breakfast on the morning of April 4, 1974. My mother was not surprised, since she knew he had serious heart issues, but she was still shocked. My parents had visited us in Redlands the previous summer and had also spent some time in a beautiful vacation setting in Palm Springs, which is less than an hour from Redlands. I went right away to be with Mom and my brothers, while Nancy and Kathy and Stephie stayed in Redlands. The funeral service was in the First Presbyterian Church in Springfield, and the burial was in the church cemetery that dated from the mid-eighteenth century.

The following summer, 1974, our family moved back to Cambridge, turning the move into a wonderful six-week cross-country adventure of visiting national parks and campgrounds: the four little piggies in their red wagon. In Cambridge we lived again in the Center for the Study of World Religions—first in Apartment 2 and then in Apartment 1 (the Director's Residence) to provide a faculty presence there during the interval between the directorships of Wilfred Cantwell Smith and John Carman. Decades later Kathy and Stephie both studied and became faculty members in anthropology because, so I and maybe even also Nancy have always thought, they had three of their formative years in a residential center of twenty-two apartments in which they were in the only family with children who were from the United States. In any case, Kathy and Stephie as well as Nancy and I relished this close community of families with kids from all over the world.

Kathy and Stephie went to school at the local public school (then known simply as Agassiz and now officially named the Maria L. Baldwin School)—which I thought was fine, while Nancy was not so sure. During those years, Nancy decided to study for a library science degree at Simmons College so that she would broaden her career options and in particular so that she would not have so many English papers to grade in and around her other duties. In the meantime, I threw myself into teaching courses in the introduction to theology, nineteenth-century Western religious thought, sociology of religion, and comparative religious worldviews. I enjoyed both my students and my colleagues—especially fellow faculty Gordon Kaufman, Dick Niebuhr, Margaret Miles, John Carman, Caroline Bynum, and Connie Buchanan. But I also became convinced that dead-end jobs were unattractive. While my appointment at Harvard was designed to cover the three years that Dick Niebuhr was on loan to the Faculty of Arts and Sciences, it was structured as a five-year contract so that I would have some flexibility in looking for a next position. I was also offered a one-semester leave as part of the contract, a leave that I decided to take as early as feasible. That turned out to be the second year of my appointment.

With a Harvard sabbatical salary (full pay for a semester) and a supplemental grant from the Association of Theological Schools for other expenses, Nancy, Kathy, Stephie, and I set off on an eight-month leave (in 1976) to live in a very small town just outside Tübingen, Germany. The town was Pfäffingen. It had a population of about 1,000, with the result that on the few occasions when we had out-of-town visitors, they could ask for us by name, and locals would respond "Oh, you mean the American family" and then give directions to our home, which was a nice little apartment that looked out over the countryside.

Kathy and Stephie attended the local school kindergarten and first grade. Both of them—at the insistence of their mother—had studied German at Saturday school not only in Boston but also in Green Bay and in Redlands. So they knew a little German. Even though Kathy was old enough to be in the second grade, Nancy and I decided to place her in the first grade so that she would learn reading and writing in German with the other starters. She flourished—assisted by a wonderful teacher who herself had lived for a year in Boston!

Stephie had a bit of a harder time at the outset. She attended a kindergarten with a teacher who did not grasp that some of her charges did not learn German as a first language. On one occasion when I went to pick her up from kindergarten, I found Stephie on the margin of the classroom crying. When I checked in with her, I learned that she was crying because she could not find the top to her water bottle. So I talked with the teacher, who replied that she had announced some time ago that the top of a water bottle had been found and asked whoever had lost it to come to claim it. I explained that Stephie was just learning German and therefore had not understood that announcement. In any case, the top to the water cap was restored! And by the time Stephie left Pfäffingen, she was fluent not only in German but in the local Schwäbisch dialect, as was her sister Kathy.

In the meantime, I engaged in research and writing, completed what would become *Beyond Existentialism and Zen: Religion in a Pluralistic World,* and then undertook further reading and research at the wonderful library of the University of Tübingen for what would become *Culture-Protestantism: German Liberal Theology at the Turn of the Twentieth Century.*

Nancy, Kathy, Stephie, and I returned to the U.S. in the summer of 1976, and as had been arranged before the leave in Germany moved back into Apartment 1 of the Center for the Study of World Religions. Both girls returned to the Agassiz School, which was within easy walking distance of the Center. Nancy took up her studies in library science with two courses each semester. I returned to my teaching and writing and participation in faculty governance, including as chair of the Department of Theology. But I also continued to feel uncomfortable in a position that was by definition a dead-end. Since my agreement with the Divinity School was that I would teach in Dick Niebuhr's place for three years and then have the luxury of two further years to explore options for the future, I felt free to begin that exploration sooner—which I did. I applied for a number of positions but found that (surprise! surprise!) there was considerable skepticism in academic circles about an associate professor of theology, even if it was at Harvard.

Still, late in the fall of 1976, I was approached by the search committee for the position of dean for Academic Affairs at the University of Wisconsin in Green Bay. There were a couple of connections that led to the approach. One was via the Danforth Foundation because some of those involved in the search had also held Danforth Graduate Fellowships. Probably more fundamental was via interest in experimental higher education. UWGB had been designated as the unit within the UW system that would explore alternative higher educational models and had a chancellor, Ed Weidner, deeply committed to multi-disciplinary curricular development. Not surprisingly there were as a result multiple relationships between Johnston College and UWGB faculty and administrators. Happily Johnston colleagues gave very positive recommendations, which led the UWGB search committee—and in particular its chair, Bob Wenger, who was a mathematician, to explore my availability.

The interviews went well. During an on-campus visit I was very impressed with the deep commitments to educational values of the UWGB students, faculty, and staff, and I also found Green Bay an intriguingly different place—one that I expected Nancy especially would appreciate as reminiscent of her New Hampshire roots. Nancy and I then made a visit together and pretty quickly decided that Green Bay would be a great place to live—maybe forever but at least until Kathy and Stephie graduated from high school! So I accepted an offer to become the dean for Academic Affairs and a professor of Humanistic Studies (since there was no religion department).

We moved in the summer of 1977. Because of pending issues at UWGB, I moved out to Green Bay about a month before Nancy, Kathy, and Stephie did. I drove our red wagon, which had no air-conditioning, and took our pets with me—an energetic little gerbil and a Peruvian guinea pig. I remember vividly that, while

driving through Chicago to stay overnight with our friends Dud
and Donna Ogle, I had a sense of panic when I thought the guinea
pig had expired! But in the end, all three of us plus some plants
arrived in Green Bay safely.

Nancy and Kathy and Stephie had a much more eventful trip.
It began with an overnight at the home of Nancy's parents in Berkeley Heights and a quick trip in to see the Statue of Liberty (since
we were leaving the East Coast before the kids had a chance to see
it!). Then the three stopped in Virginia to visit Nancy's brother
Steve and his wife Kathy and children Sheila and Scott. Steve was
then working on trade issues in the Carter Administration and
was invited to attend (with guests) the White House July 4 celebration. Nancy and Kathy and Stephanie gladly attended—and even
had the chance to shake hands with President Carter! Thereafter
they also stopped by Sea World in Ohio, which Kathy had very
much hoped to see, and after visiting the Ogles all three did man-
age to arrive in Green Bay—in time to greet John and Martha Butt,
friends from Pine Manor and Cambridge who were now living in
Minnesota and had stopped by for a visit.

For us our stay in Green Bay was a quite idyllic time. We
lived on 2827 St. Ann's Drive in a lovely red clapboard home of
about 2,000 square feet that we bought before it even went on
the market. Kathy and Stephie attended a wonderful school (the
most important reason for the appeal of this neighborhood to
us) within walking distance—and indeed they walked to it every
school day unless the temperature dropped to lower than fifteen
degrees below zero Fahrenheit, in which case one of us parents
would drive them! Each of them also developed good friendships
in the neighborhood.

Nancy decided at least for a while not to commute to Mil-
waukee to complete her library science degree and instead became
immersed in community activities, including the Union Congre-
gational Church where the whole family attended.

I became deeply engaged with my responsibilities as dean and
focused in particular on ongoing discussions of the very original
and also controversial curriculum required of all undergraduate

students. The controversy centered on whether the admittedly creative interdisciplinary courses at the core of the curriculum served more traditional students well. The disagreements were sharp because they drew on residual resentments from some of the local residents and long-term faculty who felt that the university no longer served the more vocationally oriented needs of those who in the past had flourished at UWGB when it was a local two-year community college. I also drove to Madison pretty often to represent UWGB in University of Wisconsin system-wide issues. All in all, it was a happy time for the whole family.

I got special satisfaction from working with UWGB factions, which had been deeply divided, to find common ground. In particular, in my first year as dean, an agreement was forged to reform the curriculum so that it retained its distinctive and creative multidisciplinary core but also addressed the concerns of those who felt that the initial conception of the requirements had not served some students and their faculty advocates well. By the end of the first year, the revised curriculum was designed and received approval from relevant faculty and administrative bodies. This newly articulated curriculum also proved to be helpful in cultivating better relations with what had been some dissatisfied segments of the Green Bay community. I relished working on both of those fronts.

In the summer of 1978, Nancy's parents visited us in Green Bay. It was an enjoyable time for the whole family. Nancy's father played at wrestling with Kathy and Stephie on the floor of the living room and also took walks in the fields and woods at the end of the street with his grandchildren. While he on occasion seemed very tired after such activities and talked about planning to see his doctor for a full heart check-up, he did not have major symptoms of any illness. The whole family, including Nancy's mother and siblings, were therefore completely shocked when he died suddenly and completely unexpectedly on September 21, 1978. He had a heart attack in the main terminal of Newark Airport in New Jersey and died so quickly that he never got to a hospital or even received any treatment at all, except for CPR from a physician who happened to be in the same terminal.

Nancy, Kathy, Stephie and I all attended the funeral service at the Presbyterian Church in Berkeley Heights. Then Nancy and her three brothers and sister went with their mother for the burial service in the Henniker, New Hampshire cemetery where the family had a burial plot, while I went back to Wisconsin with Kathy and Stephie.

Later in the fall of 1978, which was the family's second year in Green Bay, I was approached by Derek Bok, the then president of Harvard, to ascertain whether I could be persuaded to consider returning to Harvard Divinity School—this time as dean. It was a very attractive, yet also problematic, invitation. After extended conversations with Nancy and UWGB colleagues, I decided that I would respond positively. Following an in-person interview with Derek Bok that lasted several hours, I was offered the appointment as dean and also as the John Lord O'Brian Professor of Divinity— a tenured appointment that was especially sweet after my earlier dead-end appointment. I had long and painful discussions with my UWGB colleagues, the outcome of which was general agreement that the new opportunity was hard to decline.

In the end, with sadness at the prospect of leaving Green Bay long before the high school graduation of Kathy and Stephie and while there was still much more to do at UWGB, our family embarked on yet another move. As I noted in my message to incoming students in the fall of 1979, this was Nancy's and my fifth move to Harvard Divinity School—from New Haven, Connecticut, from Kandy, Sri Lanka, from Redlands, California, from Pfäffingen, Germany, and from Green Bay, Wisconsin. This fact alone demonstrates how powerful a magnet Harvard Divinity School was, at least for me, even over against the attractions of remaining for some further years in Green Bay.

Nancy loved Green Bay, but she was also happy or at least willing to move back to Cambridge—though she had one condition. Kathy and Stephie would not return to Agassiz but would rather apply to and attend an outstanding private school: Buckingham, Brown, and Nichols. Once that condition was settled, Nancy and I and Kathy and Stephie prepared for a further move, one complicated by the fact that it included a pet parakeet and two pet cats in the same car at the same time.

After a pleasant trip through Canada, again as four piggies (now plus pets) in their red wagon (a now nine-year-old 1970 Ford Maverick, the same one that had travelled from Cambridge to California and back), we arrived at our new home, a majestic place called Jewett House at 44 Francis Avenue, right next door to the Center for the Study of World Religions (42 Francis Avenue) and across the street from Andover Hall (45 Francis Avenue), the main building of the Divinity School.

After settling in, which included allowing three students to live in extra rooms above the kitchen in exchange for help with cooking and cleaning the huge house, Kathy and Stephie were off to school at Buckingham, Brown, and Nichols, Nancy resumed her library of science studies at Simmons, and I threw myself into my work as dean.

Because I knew the school well, I launched multiple initiatives expeditiously. Perhaps most arresting to my colleagues on the faculty was that I seized the opportunity of my first Convocation address (at the beginning of my first year as dean) to propose a thorough revision of the entire curriculum for the core master's degree programs at the heart of the school. The proposed revisions built on the historic strengths of the school but cut across some of the basic departmental divisions and also placed the study of Christianity in the context of the world religions in ways that focused more attention on the special strengths of the Center for the Study of World Religions and ties to the Faculty of Arts and Sciences. The Convocation address began a process of deliberation that included a faculty retreat and a great many task force and committee meetings. The result at the end of that first year was the formal approval of revisions that continue to shape study at the Divinity School.

Along with the revision of the curriculum, working with the budget officer at the Divinity School, I developed a computer model of the School's projected income and expenses so that the effect of modifying a range of variables could be forecast for multiple years into the future. Examples of variables include numbers of students, rates of increase in tuition, the ratio of senior to junior faculty, the level of financial aid, and the rate of increase in fundraising results. The model was quite powerful in shaping policy options—for instance, in underscoring the need to increase the ratio of junior to senior faculty—and also in impressing on the Harvard Corporation the acute need for further resources to be dedicated to the Divinity School.

An anecdote captures the power of the computer simulation. Derek Bok and the senior financial officers of the University were very impressed with the model. Consequently, Derek asked me if I would present the analysis to the Council of Deans—the heads of the ten faculties at Harvard. I did so and stimulated a vigorous discussion. On the way out the door after a stimulating set of exchanges among deans, John MacArthur, the dean of the Business School, patted me on the shoulder and remarked, "George, you don't need a computer model, you need some money." Mission accomplished! The Corporation agreed with that judgment and committed to allocating more of the University's unrestricted resources and also to helping me and my very small development staff in fundraising.

With the revised curriculum and parallel efforts in admissions and communications, the School focused sustained attention on building up the pool of applicants, which allowed a slow but steady growth in the size of the student body. That in turn supported an increase in the number of junior faculty. At the same time, the School increased its collaborations with other Harvard schools—notably the Medical School and the Kennedy School— while continuing to work closely with Arts and Sciences, in particular in the well-established joint PhD program.

All in all, the Divinity School flourished in those years. For a very long time the School was well known for its great strength in doctoral studies and research, and it continued to nurture and develop that strength. But it also achieved a much higher profile in professional education at the master's level, including but not limited to preparation for ministry. I was deeply engaged in all of that demanding process of institutional evolution, and most years I also managed to teach a seminar in the spring semester.

Nancy combined significant duties in hosting social gatherings for Divinity School students, faculty, alumni/ae, and donors with her studies in library science and her community involvements withKathy's and Stephie's education (including volunteering in the school library), the church, and other activities. She also completed her Master's of Library Science degree at Simmons. Happily, she was then offered an appointment as a librarian at Buckingham, Brown, and Nichols—an offer that she accepted with delight.

Kathy and Stephie flourished at BB&N. They enjoyed their studies and were active in extra-curricular activities ranging from sports to theater. There were of course also the challenges of growing up, including occasional struggles with friends and completing household chores. Perhaps toughest of all was a battle that Kathy had with anorexia, which to all of our great relief she managed to win.

One question that the family as a whole had to address was where to go to church. For years first Nancy and I and then the girls as well attended the Church of the Covenant in downtown Boston, a combined United Church of Christ and Presbyterian Church where our friend and eloquent preacher Joe Williamson was the pastor, together with an outstanding team of colleagues. But as Kathy and Stephanie became teenagers, there was a problem in that there were virtually no other children their age in the church community. So after considerable deliberation and quite a bit of ambivalence, we decided to switch our attendance to the University Lutheran Church, which had a solid cohort of teenagers with whom both Kathy and Stephie went through the confirmation process, and also a wonderful pastor, Fred Reisz, who has remained a good friend.

One momentous development during those years was that Kathy decided to apply for the first year of the Congress-Bundestag scholarships for American high school students to study in German secondary schools. Happily, she won the competition. So she had the opportunity to further develop her German language skills and cultivate her German friendships and connections with her German relatives.

Stephie missed her sister, but she managed to fill any extra space available with her very active and productive middle school life. In the summer following her completion of seventh grade (in 1984), our family planned a trip together to Africa—which in the end Kathy could not join because her program in Germany was starting. But I managed to schedule an extra two weeks on my way back from meetings in Thailand (including with the then-King about honoring his father, who had studied at Harvard, with a chair in Theravada Buddhism), in Pakistan, and in Kenya (at an assembly of the World Conference of Religion and Peace) for Nancy and me to celebrate our twenty-fifth wedding anniversary—and to allow Stephie to pursue her goal of climbing Mt. Kilimanjaro!

So Nancy and Stephie joined me in Nairobi, and after the conference was over, set out for the mountain—not by plane as the hotel manager insisted we should, but by matatu: a van-like vehicle filled to overflowing with local passengers. The matatu, with twenty passengers squeezed into its twelve seats, headed from Nairobi for the Kenya-Tanzania border, dropping off and picking up passengers along the way. At that point, it was necessary to walk through security gates on both sides of the border and then get on to a Tanzanian bus that was filling with Maasai warriors. When we were seated and about to leave, a little girl in the seat in front of us turned around, looked at Stephie, and started to scream. Her mother calmed her down and explained that she had never before seen a white person and was afraid. In any case, after switching buses at the nearest market town, we three travelers found our way to the hotel that served as the base camp for climbers. The climb was well-guided but was very arduous—three and a half days up and a day and a half back.

A huge disappointment, which in the end only fueled her appetite for returning to Africa, was that Stephie had to stop at the last shelter before the final ascent because she could not stop throwing up even when she had nothing left in her stomach. She was thirteen at the time, which we later learned is often too young to have the cardiac capacity for climbing to the very top (over 19,000 feet). Nancy and I did struggle to the top while Stephie waited with a guide at about 15,000 feet. It will not surprise anyone who knows Stephie that she took the very next opportunity she had, which was with our good friends Bud and Donna Ogle two years later, to undertake the climb again, that time all the way to the top.

During the year that Kathy was in Germany (1984–85), another disruption of shared plans occurred. I was approached by the search committee for the presidency of Rice University. I told the chair of the committee, Ralph O'Connor, three different times that I was not interested because the timing just did not work for both family and job reasons. On the family side, Nancy and I felt that we could not ask Kathy, when she came back from her year in Germany, to attend her senior year of high school in a new school in a completely new city. As far as job responsibilities, I was in the midst of negotiations with the Harvard Corporation for a substantial increase in support for the Divinity School. But the search committee did not take those reasons to be dispositive and enlisted another member to press the matter. Bill Martin, who had completed his PhD in the same program that I had been in, called and said simply, "George, you are being closed-minded; you have never even seen the university that you are turning down." After some back and forth, the search committee and I agreed that Nancy and I would undertake a completely confidential visit.

Nancy and I were about to go on a fundraising trip to California and decided we could paste in a few days for a stopover in Houston. I decided to tell no one at Harvard about the stopover in Houston except for Derek Bok. Derek was not surprised and said that the search committee had met with him and that he had recommended me very positively—after noting that he thought Harvard had hidden me pretty well over there in the Divinity School!

At the hotel in Houston, Nancy and I were booked as Mr. and Mrs. Kentucky (the renowned basketball coach at the University of Kentucky was Adolph Rupp) and indeed seemed completely anonymous except to the members of the search committee. Nancy and I were both very impressed with Rice and also with what we saw of Houston. The campus was magnificent but even more attractive was the sense of excitement about launching a new era in the history of the university after the fifteen years of stabilization under the current president. Upon his return, I felt obliged to report to Derek Bok that the prospect of moving to Rice was not as out-of-the-question as I had thought before the visit.

In the next weeks, several Rice trustees whom I had not yet met came to Cambridge to visit, and discussions continued. At the same time, negotiations with the Harvard Corporation had reached solid enough ground that I no longer felt the situation of the Divinity School would be severely disadvantaged if the next stage of its leadership were to be a new dean.

At this point, Ralph O'Connor seized the initiative again. In a phone conversation, he told me that he was tired of hearing about the daughter in Germany and the challenge she would face if she had to move for her senior year. He suggested that I fly to Germany (at Rice's expense) and discuss the prospect with her. He also asked that I take along some documents that would be provided, including literature about Saint John's School, an outstanding private school, and also Bellaire High School, the language magnet school of the Houston Independent School District.

Though we were clear with each other that Kathy would not have a veto power over our decision, Nancy and I agreed that the prospect of moving to Rice was intriguing enough to warrant a trip to Germany for a discussion with her that included the school options that Ralph had suggested. This time, because the prospect was no longer so far-fetched, I decided that, in addition to informing Derek Bok, I should also have a talk with the faculty council, an informal advisory group of three colleagues that I had established for discreet counsel on pending issues.

As I walked in the door of the home where Kathy was living during her year in Germany, the phone was ringing. The call was for me. It was Derek Bok, who reported that he had just met with a delegation of faculty from the Divinity School who were extremely distressed that I was considering resigning from the deanship. Derek asked that I make no final decision until the two of us had a chance to talk further and set the morning of my return from the quick trip to Germany as the time for that discussion.

Kathy and I had time for a lot of intense conversation during an afternoon and evening of long walks and extended talk in the home where she was living. The outcome of those deliberations was Kathy's definite conclusion that the family should not stay in Cambridge just so that she could complete her studies at Buckingham, Brown, and Nichols. She even ventured that she might welcome the new experience, because if she were to return to BB&N, she would not have the kind of leadership positions she might have had if she had not been away for her junior year. Instead of being a bit of an outsider in Cambridge, moving to Houston would be like the excitement of a further year abroad before she went off to college.

She was also especially intrigued with the yearbook of the Bellaire High School, with page after page of photographs of the students at the school—the Chinese Club, the Hebrew Club, the Spanish Club, the French Club, the Korean Club and so on. The conclusion was clear: Kathy would be happy to stay in Cambridge, but she also would not at all be averse to moving to Houston, which meant that her situation should no longer be an obstacle to relocating.

The morning after I returned from Germany, I met with Derek Bok, who was quite emphatic in arguing for the Cambridge rather than the Houston alternative. He noted that none of his deans had left before the ten years of appointment that he considered the norm. He also insisted that there would be lots of other opportunities in outstanding colleges and universities—at which point I could not resist pointing out that Derek's northeast provincialism was showing. In any case, after an extended and mutually supportive conversation, I said that I would consider all of the points made further but that I was increasingly open to the Rice overture.

The next step was to report to Ralph O'Connor about the trip to talk with Kathy. He was of course pleased to hear that this obstacle to considering the prospect of Rice and Houston in the family's future was no longer insurmountable, and he proposed that a small subset of the search committee and a few trustees come to

Cambridge to visit with Nancy and me. The visit was scheduled over a weekend and proved to be a very engaging set of discussions. In the course of the visit, Ralph had a side conversation with Stephie in which he asked her if she liked the thought of having a horse—and, if so, what her preferred color was! Nancy and I had worried much less about the impact of a move on Stephie than on Kathy, because she would in any case be finishing middle school and would therefore be starting a new chapter in her education. (Little did we know!) In any case, as it turned out, Ralph and Stephie continued to be close for decades afterward. Following this visit with Rice leaders, a formal offer was forthcoming, and after further discussion, Nancy and I decided to accept it.

Left to right: Prescott Farrar, Katherine (Polly) Farrar, Nancy, George,
Erika Braunöhler Rupp, Gustav Wilhelm Rupp.
Wedding of Nancy and George, New Jersey, 1964.

Left to right: George, Kathy, Stephie, Nancy.
At home in Redlands, California, 1972.

Left to right: Stephie, Kathy. At home in Redlands, California, 1971.

Left to right: Nancy, Stephie (holding Chutney), Kathy, George, Wyoming, 1985.

Left to right: Erika Rupp, Katherine Farrar, Nancy, Kathy, Stephie, and George. In the yard of the Rice President's House, Texas, 1991.

Left to right: Stephie, George, Kathy, Paolo Coppi, Nancy.
Wedding of Kathy and Paolo, Chicago, 1993.

Left to right: Ben Kwek, Shin Kwek, Ju-Hon Kwek, Stephie, Nancy, and
George. Reception for the wedding of Stephanie and Ju-Hon,
Singapore, 2000.

Front: Polly Farrar (holding Bonnie); left to right in back: Charles, Joanne, John, Steve, and Nancy. Nancy's mother and siblings, New Hampshire, 1996.

Left to right: George, Nancy, Kathy, and Stephanie.
Building our boat house, Trumbull, Connecticut, 1997.

Front row, left to right: Erika Rupp, Ruth Braunöhler Schulte; middle row,
left to right: Stephanie, Kathy, Nancy, Jean Rupp, Marie Rupp, Erin Rupp;
back row, left to right: Paolo Coppi, George, Herb Rupp, and Pete Rupp.
Family reunion, Virginia, 1997.

Back row, left to right: George, Alex Rupp-Coppi, Leo Rupp-Coppi,
Paolo Coppi; middle row, left to right: Nancy, Erika Rupp-Coppi, Kathy,
Kai-Shan Kwek-Rupp, Stephanie, Kai-Lin Kwek-Rupp, Ju-Hon Kwek;
front at right: Kai-Jin Kwek-Rupp.
Family reunion, Trumbull, Connecticut, 2019.

Third Quarter

Houston and New York

(1985–2002)

LEAVING ALL OF THE connections in Cambridge and the Boston area was certainly difficult. All four members of our immediate family have stayed in contact with friends from Cambridge and Boston, especially Nancy who has been instrumental in maintaining relations with four families with whom she and I have spent many joyous vacations and shorter visits. Still, Nancy not only was moving from close contacts with good friends, but also from her valued position as a librarian at a great school. For Stephie the move was made slightly easier because the family acquired a wonderful new dog—bred by Nancy's brother, Uncle John—to whom the whole family became devoted. Her name was Chutney, and she was all but inseparable from Stephie during the moving process. For Kathy the move was a bit easier because she had already been separated from her friends for the year she was in Germany. I comforted myself based both on what I knew was Nancy's skill of keeping in touch and also what I was confident would remain professional connections with colleagues.

Houston was in significant ways a new beginning for all four of us. Kathy would start at Bellaire High School, the magnet language program for the whole Houston Independent School

District that also offered the International Baccalaureate diploma program (a fact that would provide a significant touchstone decades later when I became involved with the IB). She was ready to become involved with the international programs at Bellaire—and also to begin the process of applying to colleges.

Stephie was less enamored about attending her new school because she missed Cambridge enormously. The school was an outstanding private institution that regularly sent its graduates to outstanding colleges and universities: St. John's School. Nancy's and my sense that starting as a freshman at a new high school would be an easier adjustment than joining as a senior turned out to be a misplaced confidence, since Stephie had been looking forward to continuing her education with her friends at Buckingham, Brown, and Nichols even if it would be on a new campus. It took a while for her to come to terms with her new situation—though she was helped in her adjustment to life in Texas by her wonderful dog Chutney and also Del-Rio Cody, the horse that Ralph O'Connor had promised her as an inducement in the closing phase of the search!

As for Nancy, she had in the meantime secured appointment as a librarian at St. John's School. There were of course the demands of moving into a new home and organizing a whole range of personal affairs and public entertaining. While Nancy certainly bore the brunt of those demands, we all shared in settling in to a life together that continued positive patterns from previous places—including the red wagon (our then fifteen-year-old Ford Maverick) that would be the vehicle with which both Kathy and Stephie would learn to drive.

As is my custom, I threw myself fully into the challenges and opportunities that a new setting offered. I spent time getting to know my new colleagues and was delighted with the eagerness to move Rice forward that almost all of them seemed to share. It was a wonderful institution with a great history and identity—and it could build on that heritage to become even much more. Over time there would be changes in the leadership team, but for starters a great cohort was ready to move ahead.

One unanticipated continuity became clear on the first day that I was in my office in early July of 1985. Brother Pete called to inform his little brother and his family that he and his wife Marie and their daughter Erin would also be moving to Houston! He had just learned that he would be transferred from New Jersey to Texas. He had worked with Exxon during summers when he was a student at M.I.T. and then full-time since his graduation from the University of Chicago Business School. After living in Louisiana and New Jersey, he was now being transferred to Houston, the hometown of his wife Marie. Completely unexpectedly, there would therefore be a larger collection of Rupps in Houston, which meant that three cousins would be close to each other geographically and that in particular Stephie and Erin, who were almost exactly the same age, could see each other much more regularly than would otherwise be the case.

By the time of my official inauguration in October of 1985, there was considerable excitement about the years ahead. In my inaugural address, I sketched an overall agenda that built on what I saw as the historical strengths of the university. I had invited two university presidents who were colleagues and friends to join the ceremony and the lavish dinner afterward: Jim Laney, the president of Emory University, and Derek Bok, the president of Harvard.

Jim was a long-time friend from when he and his wife Berta and Nancy and I all were at Yale together; he was a bit older and was completing a PhD after working as a missionary and teacher in Korea for a decade. He had also lived briefly with Nancy and me in the Center for the Study of World Religions while he was on a sabbatical before assuming the presidency of Emory. In regard to Rice, Jim had been the first person to recommend me to the search committee when it met with him.

In contrast, Derek had been very skeptical about my going to Rice and had tried hard to persuade me not to go. Yet he graciously agreed to attend the inauguration and to speak at the inaugural dinner. Both Jim and Derek added greatly to the occasion. But what was most striking is that after returning to Cambridge, Derek wrote me a letter in which he noted simply that he had been wrong in seeking to dissuade me from going and that he could now see why I had found the opportunity to be compelling.

While leaders in place were eager to be part of the next Rice chapter, two key ones had previously announced their intention to retire from their positions: the provost and the dean of the Wiess School of Natural Sciences—two critically important and visible sets of responsibilities. I focused quickly on the searches for successors in those positions, which I knew colleagues would view as a signal of the values and orientation of the new president. National searches conducted through search committees staffed with leading faculty members and a few students led to two terrific recruitments. The new provost, who would become my closest colleague, was Neal Lane, a physicist who had left Rice only two years earlier to become the Chancellor of the University of Colorado campus in Colorado Springs but was excited to return with the promise of a more concentrated and intentional commitment to moving the University forward to more fully realizing its potential. The new dean of Sciences was Jim Kinsey, a Rice alumnus and chemistry professor who was serving as dean of Sciences at M.I.T. Success in recruiting two very distinguished scientists who also had deep awareness of and attachment to Rice was deemed a very promising sign.

Other resignations (some of which I admittedly encouraged) soon allowed further recruitments: a new dean for the Shepherd School of Music, Michael Hammond, who came from the State University of New York in Purchase, where he was president, and was attracted to my publicly stated insistence that if Rice were to have a school of music, it would have to be an excellent one, which meant building a great new facility rather than being housed in nooks and crannies around the campus; a new dean of of the George R. Brown School of Engineering, Michael Carroll, who came to Rice from the role of dean of Engineering at the University of California, Berkeley; and a new vice president for Finance and Administration, Dean Currie, who came to Rice from his role as associate dean at the Harvard Business School.

Along with building a strong leadership team, I also undertook substantive initiatives. Two are illustrative. The first was a revision of the undergraduate curriculum. Rice is distinctive among leading American universities in having just about half of its undergraduates major in the sciences and engineering and the other half in the arts, humanities, and social sciences—in contrast to, for example, M.I.T. and Cal Tech on the one hand (where the vast majority of students concentrate in the sciences and engineering) and Ivy League colleges on the other (where most students major in the arts, humanities, and social sciences). With the leadership of Neal Lane, a plan was developed and approved that required majors on either side of this "two cultures" divide to have a "coherent minor" on the other side, a distinctive curricular structure that expressed the unusual student and faculty composition that I saw as a defining characteristic of Rice.

The second example is in the area of research. I was attracted to and intrigued by the small scale of Rice: fewer than 4,000 students (about 2600 undergraduate and 1200 graduate students) and about 400 faculty. But this small scale could be a disadvantage in competing for major research funding. (To get a sense of the contrast, I checked how many faculty members were in a given field in major research universities. To summarize the difference in one admittedly extreme instance, the University of California, Berkeley, had more faculty members in its department of biology than the total of Rice faculty.) Rice had one very distinguished research area that pulled together faculty from chemistry, physics, chemical and electrical engineering, and mathematics. It was named the Rice Quantum Institute and was chaired by Rick Smalley, who a decade later would be awarded the Nobel Prize in Chemistry for his path-breaking research in nano science based in the Rice Quantum Institute. This multidisciplinary institute became the model for a handful of such institutes that in effect made a virtue of Rice's relatively small scale by drawing investigators form multiple areas to collaborate across conventional boundaries and thereby design programs and attract funding for which other more disciplinarily defined programs were less competitive.

Nancy was also very fully occupied between hosting lots of Rice occasions at the President's House, and then in the middle of our first year in Houston with the position she was offered and accepted as a librarian at St. John's School. Kathy, too, was very busy between settling in at her school, applying to colleges, and working at a part-time job in a bagel bakery and shop, the "Bagel Manufactuary" in Rice Village, the small commercial area just off campus. Stephie started ninth grade. While we had hoped that transition would be a more or less easy point at which to integrate into a new school, it turned out to be pretty tough, in part because Stephie missed her life in Cambridge so much. It took a while, but she soon made close friends, with some of whom she continues to be in contact, and was able to run track and play soccer, in addition to doing well in her studies.

Nancy and I became quite engaged in multiple aspects of life in Houston. In addition to hosting Rice-connected dinners and receptions, there were also a great many interactions with the broader Houston community. In Nancy's case, those connections developed from her contacts in the library and education worlds and also extended to long-term friendships with faculty and faculty spouses and members of reading groups and all the others whom Nancy met and with whom she then nurtured connections.

For my part, I got involved with a wide range of organizations. Through Rice, I became a member of the Association of Texas College and Universities (and over time its vice president and then president), the Association of American Universities, the Houston Advanced Research Center (HARC), and the Council on Research and Technology (CORTECH). I served on the Rhodes Scholarship selection committee for the Southwest region. I also became quite involved with the Forum Club of Houston and served on its executive committee and then for terms as president and chairperson. I was as well a member of the boards of the Houston Symphony, the Greater Houston Partnership, the United Way of the Texas Gulf Coast, the Marian and Speros Martel Foundation (through Ralph O'Connor), the Methodist Hospital, Amigos de las Americas, and St. John's School (after Nancy was well established there, though before Stephie graduated). I also for the first time served on the boards of for-profit companies: the Panhandle Eastern Corporation (courtesy of the vice chair of the Rice Board, Josephine Abercrombie) and the Texas Commerce Bank–Houston.

Even before the move to Houston, I received numerous invitations to preach or give talks at churches from all over Texas. I pretty quickly decided that I would either be the president of Rice or the fill-in preacher and adult education speaker for the Houston area. So that I would be able to be the former and rather than the latter, I decided early-on to decline all such invitations—so that no one could be offended that I declined some while accepting others. Then friends, who had some sense of my religious orientation, also advised that I not transfer my Presbytery membership from Boston to Houston to avoid any uproar from more conservative members of the Houston Presbytery. Because Kathy and Stephie had both been confirmed in the University Lutheran Church in Cambridge, we included Christ the King Lutheran Church (a block from the Rice campus) in those we visited when we were looking for a church home—along with the First Presbyterian Church of Houston (a few blocks from the Rice campus). In the end the unanimous vote of the family was for the Lutherans over the Calvinists!

There were down points for our family in the Rice years. That Stephie's adjustment to the move was tougher than Nancy and I had anticipated was one downer. Another was a terrible accident in which another dog clawed out the eye of Chutney, leaving her the most wonderful one-eyed woofer in the world, yet still with only one eye for the rest of her life! A third was the selling of the red wagon that had served us so faithfully for over sixteen years (and had a few rocky escapades during the driver education of Kathy in particular). Happily, none of these setbacks was insurmountable.

Overall, the Rice years were positive for our family, even for the member who was there the shortest time. Kathy went off to college at Princeton after her one year at Bellaire. Before leaving Kathy talked with us about her interest in learning another language in addition to the English and German in which she was fluent. She was weighing Chinese and Japanese. In one of the worst bits of advice I have ever given, I recommended Japanese. I ac knowledged that in the long run Chinese would be of enormous value, but I also argued that, by the time she finished her bachelor's degree or even her PhD if she went on to graduate school, Chinese would not yet be as crucial as it no doubt would be in decades to come. That advice was given in 1986: Japan's economy was then enormously powerful and not yet obviously moving toward decades of stagnation, whereas China was not yet exercising much global influence. In any case, certainly not based on that advice alone, Kathy went through the enormous struggle of learning Japanese, which included an exciting year at the Stanford Center in Kyoto, where Nancy and I had the pleasure of visiting her.

During those years Stephie developed friendships (with boys as well as girls) that were very positive and constructive. She also developed bonds through her athletic ability in both soccer and cross-country running. (One event that she prefers not to mention was a daddy-daughter soccer match-up in which we dads unexpectedly won!) She enjoyed as well the companionship of Chutney and riding her horse Del-Rio Cody, though she had less and less time for that as she became more deeply immersed in school activities and finally reluctantly gave him back to Ralph O'Connor.

But as involved as she became with her Houston activities, she also looked forward to getting back to the Northeast. When it became time to apply to college, she focused on Dartmouth, and when she was admitted, she was excited about returning to hills and snow. At Dartmouth, Stephie was torn between pre-medical studies and the social sciences. Spending her junior year in Africa—first in Kenya and then traveling more broadly—attracted her decisively to anthropology, in which she majored and did very well.

Nancy enjoyed her work at St. John's both before and after Stephie graduated and also as perennial hostess and friend of everyone at Rice. She met regularly with a small group of friends and has kept in close touch with them over the years. Whenever Nancy and I have occasion to visit Rice or Houston, a reunion celebration with this group is always a highpoint of the trip.

There was great progress at Rice. The spirit among students and faculty was high. A broad range of initiatives raised the profile of the University. Research funding increased markedly, as did revenues from fundraising. Perhaps most remarkable was the enormous increase in applications for undergraduate admission. I have enjoyed noting that in my final year at Rice the applications for admission included more Merit Scholar finalists than there were places in the incoming class—including a greatly increased number from outside Texas as well as from Texas itself. Among many efforts to raise Rice's profile nationally and even internationally, perhaps the most successful was hosting of the 1988 Economic Summit, which brought round-the-clock publicity not only across the U.S. but also in Europe and Japan.

Yet I was also convinced that for Rice to maintain the forward momentum evident across the university, it was crucial to generate new sources of revenue. Support for research had increased substantially. Tuition income had also increased, but it was crucial for the historic identity of Rice to keep charges to students as low as feasible and to provide generous financial aid. Especially corrected for the size of the student body, the existing Rice endowment was very substantial—but it could not be relied on as the backstop for all initiatives. I therefore felt strongly that Rice should do what it had never done seriously since its founding: launch a major campaign for new capital to augment its endowment, and do so from the position of financial and academic strength that it occupied. There was widespread support for such an initiative—among faculty, alumni/ae, and the board. I indicated that if a campaign were to be launched in the coming year or two, I would be prepared to commit to remaining for five years to see it through to a successful conclusion.

In the spring of 1992 a board retreat was held to finalize plans for this major capital campaign. There was strong support for moving forward with the plan, which had an initial modest goal of two hundred fifty million dollars. The retreat was a demanding but on the whole also very upbeat three days. Then on the Monday morning after the retreat, the chair of the board, Charles Duncan, visited me in my office with the stern message that, despite the good spirits at the retreat, there would be no capital campaign. One trustee, who all thought would be a major donor to any successful campaign, had in effect vetoed the move—with the acquiescence of Charles and one other board member. Charles and I had an hour of very intense conversation. At the end of it, Charles said, "George, you have no choice: there will be no campaign." I replied that I would think about the conversation, talk with Nancy about it, and then get back to Charles the next morning.

It is not a good strategy to tell me that I have no choice. Upon reflection and in conversation with Nancy, I concluded that I could do Rice more good by resigning than by staying on after this rejection of my recommendation of a capital campaign. The need for these new funds from grateful alumni/ae would sooner or later be recognized by all Rice constituencies. Indeed, it was already widely embraced. I decided that I would resign, that I would continue to work diligently through the 1992–93 academic year, that I would do all that I could to help in finding a good successor, and that I would one way or another move on to new opportunities, though I had no idea what those might be (other than staying on as a professor at Rice, which my tenured faculty appointment would allow). The next morning I went to visit Charles in his office and informed him of this decision.

Charles was taken aback. He called an emergency board meeting, which almost all of the board attended in person or by phone. I explained why I thought I could serve Rice better by leaving than by staying under the circumstances of having what I deemed a central priority rejected. Intense and eloquent support was voiced for me and for the plan to raise funds. But in the end, my decision to resign effective the end of the 1992–93 academic year remained in place.

Because Rice is very prominent in Houston and the Rice community is very close-knit, there was no way this series of events would remain private. I needed to inform my senior team of my decision, which I did, much to their distress. Faculty, staff, and students also soon learned of the transition that would be under way. My resignation became front-page news in the Houston newspapers. There was a lot of unhappiness, but also a resolve to move on for the best outcome achievable for all constituents. I expressed and strongly supported that resolve.

I did indeed continue to work diligently during my final year at Rice. As the search committee for my successor conducted its work, it kept me informed and enlisted me when it was appropriate—including in helping to recruit Malcolm Gillis, who became my successor. I also began to hear from search committees for other positions.

Ironically, Yale and Columbia were both looking for new presidents during the 1992–93 academic year. In the case of Yale, I had earlier in the summer declined to be considered, but with the new developments, the search committee again approached me—and this time I was indeed willing to be considered. Columbia also approached me. I had interviews with both search committees. I had a connection to Yale in that I was an alumnus (admittedly of the Divinity School, which was a somewhat dubious base for many Yalies). In contrast, I had no Columbia connections—which was true of no Columbia president except for Dwight Eisenhower, who was president of Columbia briefly before running for president of the U.S. in 1952.

In the interviews I had during the Yale search, it was clear that search committee members had a very hard time accepting the conflict that I had with the Rice board. In contrast, the Columbia search committee was very interested in the conflict with the board, but did not become obsessed with it. In the end, when Columbia offered me the position despite my lack of previous Columbia connections, and I accepted it, the chair of the board at Columbia, who was also the chair of the presidential search committee, Henry King, responded forthrightly when asked in the news conference about the conflict. He indicated that the search committee was of course very interested in this conflict, examined it very thoroughly, and came to the conclusion that my position in the disagreement was entirely defensible, indeed seemed right.

I continued to be very close to my colleagues at Rice, including many board members. The closing of the conflict between me and the Rice board was perhaps most dramatically confirmed in the fall of 1993 in a meeting in the Columbia president's office. A delegation of the Rice board visited me in my office to seek my counsel as they mounted a major capital campaign. This remarkably different position was the result of changes in the leadership of the board during further deliberations about a capital campaign. Striking was the fact that the goal of the new campaign was to be five hundred million dollars—twice the level that I had proposed a year earlier. It should also be noted that this goal was achieved and that since then, under president David Leebron (whom I had appointed dean of Columbia Law School and had recommended to Rice during the search for the successor to Malcolm Gillis), a further one billion-dollar campaign was also successfully concluded. I appreciated my visit with the Rice delegation, and I congratulated them on the initiative they were embracing.

In any case, I worked assiduously to assure a smooth transition to my successor as president, Malcolm Gillis, even as Nancy and I began the process of relocation to New York. This process occurred during a summer in which our family celebrated two crucial events: first, Stephie's commencement from Dartmouth; and second, the marriage of Kathy and Paolo Coppi. The timing was tough in the midst of also moving, but both occasions were wonderful. Stephie's graduation was a characteristically celebratory and enjoyable occasion, and so was the wedding of Kathy and Paolo.

Kathy had relocated to Chicago after her commencement from Princeton to pursue her PhD at the leading anthropology department in the country. Paolo was a post-doctoral fellow in astrophysics at the University of Chicago upon completing his undergraduate degree at Harvard and his PhD at Cal Tech. He is the son of Bruno and Maria Coppi, both immigrants from Italy who met when they were scholars at the Institute for Advanced Studies in Princeton. Kathy and Paolo in turn met through friends and pretty quickly decided to marry. It was an honor and a joy to be involved in the wedding, which included our good friend Bud

Ogle as officiant in a ceremony that incorporated both Catholic and Protestant motifs—and also the visual presence of Buddhism through the robe worn by one of Kathy's colleagues. The decision to celebrate their wedding in Chicago was both because it was convenient for their friends and fellow students and faculty and also because the parents of the bride were between homes!

After the family celebrations and reunions during the summer, Kathy and Stephie took the next steps that seemed right for them. Kathy returned to her graduate studies in anthropology at the University of Chicago and Paolo to his research in astrophysics, also at the University of Chicago. Stephie worked in Hanover for an additional semester in the environmental lab of one of her mentors before returning to Africa, this time to the Ituri Forest (in the former Zaire) for six months of work with the Wildlife Conservation Society. Then she moved to Cambridge for a master's in education program at Harvard.

With our daughters fully occupied in their own pursuits, Nancy and I settled in to a new chapter of our lives at Columbia. Nancy decided that she preferred not to continue her work as a librarian and instead would focus on the hosting and entertainment roles that she and I both felt were crucial—and for which Columbia offered her a modest stipend. As is her custom, Nancy also engaged in social circles of her own. Perhaps the one that has continued the longest is a book group of New York-based professionals who meet each month to discuss a book that all members read and that is then the focus of a discussion led by one of them. When Nancy joined, the group had already been meeting for fifteen years, first in Washington and then in New York. It is still meeting—and about to celebrate its fortieth anniversary. Nancy began to meet with the group during the Columbia years and has continued to attend virtually every meeting since then, even when doing so entails a five-hour round-trip commute from Trumbull to New York City and back to Trumbull.

Our new home was the President's House at Columbia. The house itself was a big challenge: built in 1912, it comprises 17,000 square feet that for years had been used only for entertainment because the previous president of Columbia had lived in his own off-campus residence. Faced with Columbia's daunting financial challenges, I decided that minimal renovations would have to do to make the third floor livable as a residence—with the aim of more basically renovating the entire six floors as resources allowed.

The financial challenges Columbia faced extended far beyond the President's House. The year before my arrival, the University had an annual operating budget deficit of seventy million dollars, a clearly unsustainable shortfall. There were also serious morale problems—evident, for example, in the faculty vote of no confidence in Michael Sovern, my predecessor as president. So the opening year of my presidency required significant cuts in the operating budget at the very time that student and faculty morale had to be rebuilt.

I decided to recruit a faculty task force to engage with the administration on the best ways to bring the budget back into balance. Working with Provost Jonathan Cole (a long-term Columbian since his undergraduate education at the College and his PhD from the graduate school), I appointed a university-wide task force to focus priorities and to begin the process of restructuring the budget to allow significant reductions without undermining central educational and research commitments. I named David Auston, the dean of the School of Engineering and Applied Sciences, as chair of this task force, based on his work as chair of the budget committee of a strategic planning commission that had just completed its work.

At the same time I launched the process of building a new leadership team in the Arts and Sciences—a team that would integrate more effectively the work of the schools within the Arts and Sciences. This process in the end entailed appointing a new vice president for the Arts and Sciences and new deans for Columbia College, the School of General Studies, and the Graduate School of Arts and Sciences. In an unprecedented move intended to institutionalize the centrality of undergraduate education at Columbia, I appointed the same person, Steven Marcus, to be both dean of the College and vice president for the Arts and Sciences and to work closely as a kind of troika with the dean of General Studies, Caroline Bynum, and the dean of the Graduate School, Eduardo Macagno, to achieve greater integration and joint setting of priorities. All three were long-term Columbia faculty members, and in Steven Marcus' case, with a bachelor's degree from Columbia College and a PhD from the graduate school.

I began the process of shaping a new administrative team as well. Recognizing the urgent need for more effective control of the finances and the management of the university, I recruited John Masten from the New York Public Library to be executive vice president for Finance and Emily Lloyd from her position as New York City Sanitation Commissioner to be executive vice president for Administration. Soon to follow was a new vice president for Public Affairs, Alan Stone, who came from Washington with the experience of senior staff roles in both Congress and the White House.

While there was quite a bit of turmoil through these changes, which included the departure of a number of long-established administrative personnnel, considerable progress was also soon evident. The Auston taskforce worked closely with me and the central administration to develop recommendations to bring the budget back into balance, a goal that was soon achieved with overall agreement despite unavoidable budget reductions. At the same time, I worked closely with the Development Department to relaunch and elevate systematic fundraising efforts, in particular focused on the core budget of the arts and sciences. Fortunately, the leaders of the Development Department, Ann McSweeney and Richard Naum, were deeply experienced, knew the various constituencies well, and were very willing, even eager, to enlist me and work with me in such efforts.

Fundraising results offer a convenient metric of the forward movement achieved. Columbia was in the midst of a one-billion-dollar capital campaign, publicly launched in 1990 and with a total raised of about five hundred million dollars when I took office. During my middle years in office, the goal was increased to two billion dollars. By the time I resigned, the amount raised was $2.84 billion—a total that has been surpassed since then but that was a record for a university at the time. A similar pattern is evident in total funds raised, whether for the capital campaign or for annual expenses—known as "current use" funds. For the nine years of my presidency, the totals of those funds rose each year compared to the year before and therefore were a record each time, from $116.2 million in 1992–93 (the year before I assumed office) to $358.7 million in 2000–2001, when I announced that I would be leaving.

With the achievement of a balanced budget and the prospect over time of substantially increased fundraising results, the stage was set for advances on the priorities that I had set in my inaugural address: to establish undergraduate education as a central priority for the university as a whole; to improve Columbia's relationship with its local communities, Morningside Heights, Harlem, and Washington Heights as well as with New York City as a whole; and to raise further Columbia's profile as a global university. We pursued those priorities assiduously for my nine years as president.

Enhancing undergraduate education and also focusing more attention on the value of a small undergraduate student population in a great university and a global city required major new investments in core facilities: a new and much improved student center; a major renovation of the central library; upgraded dormitories and athletic facilities; and new residential facilities. As important was more effectively communicating the strengths of the undergraduate education offered and in particular the advantages of being located in New York City. One measure of success in this set of tasks is the fact that over nine years the number of applications to Columbia College more than doubled, and the percentage of applicants accepted became more competitive with acceptances going from the top 30.3% to the top 12.2%.

Along with this attention to enhancing undergraduate education, I also worked to improve relations with neighboring communities. I became personally acquainted with local leaders and strongly encouraged a range of community service activities both by students and through curricular developments in particular in the School of Architecture. In the final years of my time as president, I also led the effort to build support for a Columbia expansion into the neighborhood north of the university, Manhattanville. After extensive discussions with the community board responsible for that neighborhood and also with elected political leaders, there was broad-based support for an expansion of the Columbia footprint that would serve both the university and neighboring communities. As a result, it was with community support that Columbia proceeded to buy more of the property north of the campus to supplement what was already owned—acquiring virtually all of it prior to my leaving office.

I also invested considerable time and energy in building further on Columbia's well-established reputation as an international university. Those efforts included travel to alumni gatherings abroad, visits with global leaders, cultivating connections with United Nations agencies, and further developing the resources of all Columbia schools and especially of the School for International Affairs for global programming. It also resulted in the creation of an international advisory council, co-chaired by John Kluge and David Rockefeller, that included members from every continent.

There were of course innumerable initiatives across the university during these nine years, especially as research funding increased substantially and as unrestricted income from patents that the University owned grew even more rapidly. New and renovated facilities both on Morningside Heights and in the Washington Heights were steadily launched and completed, as were curricular revisions and collaborations across schools and disciplines. Vice Provost Michael Crow and Provost Jonathan Cole were especially active in encouraging such initiatives.

A vibrant example of such cross-disciplinary and cross-school programs was the establishment of the Columbia Earth Institute, which connected university-wide programs that addressed environmental issues and enabled us to recruit Jeffrey Sachs from Harvard as its first director. But even with this broad array of new initiatives, the nine years of my presidency were still centered on enhancing undergraduate education, connecting constructively with neighboring communities, and continuing to raise the profile of Columbia as a global university.

Nancy and I also continued to be engaged with other associations and organizations. While at Rice, we had become supporters of Bread for the World, a Christian advocacy organization dedicated to generating support for the alleviation of poverty both in the U.S. and abroad. In time, Nancy became a member of the Bread board, and I became the founding chair of the Alliance to End Hunger, a new organization that Bread for the World launched in order to build a coalition among all faith-based groups that were advocates for addressing the needs of poor people around the globe.

Because Columbia, like Rice, was a member of the Association of American Universities, I continued to be active in it and served a term as chairperson. I also joined the boards of a broad range of other organizations: BIO Ventures for Global Health; Campus Compact (including a term on its executive committee); CASA, the National Center on Addiction and Substance Abuse (a Columbia affiliate); the Cathedral of St. John the Divine (a Columbia neighbor); the Commission of Independent Colleges and Universities; the Committee for Economic Development (for which I co-chaired a subcommittee that reported on and advocated for political campaign finance reform); the Consortium on Financing Higher Education; the Council on Foreign Relations (including some years later a term on its board); the Freedom Forum Media Studies Center; IDT Capital; the Institute of International Education; the National Association of Independent Colleges and Universities; the Presbyterian Hospital; and the Pulitzer Prize board.

As I moved into the second semester of my eighth year at Columbia, I decided that the timing was right for a transition. The Campaign for Columbia had closed at almost triple its initial target. Major building projects were completed or nearing completion. Morale was positive all around. Furthermore, I figured I had one career move left, which would be less true if I waited a few years to move from my current position. I therefore informed Steve Friedman, the chair of the board, that I would like to announce my resignation so that there could be a careful search for my successor, with the goal of a transition in the summer of 2002. The board was quite resistant to this news and tried to convince me that staying in office for at least a few more years would be better. I insisted that sooner was advisable in order to maintain the momentum under way. To maintain that momentum, further major funding would be required. A new president would need to have a year or two to settle into the role, get to know the various constituencies, and only then could plan and launch a new campaign. After considerable discussion, it was agreed that I would announce my resignation and that a serious search for my successor would be launched by late spring.

While I did not know what I would do next, I felt that I could not be a responsible and effective leader if I quietly explored other options without first announcing my plans to resign. But once it was pubic knowledge that I planned to leave, I could begin the process of seeing what might make sense for a next position. I began by conferring with long-term colleagues and friends.

Perhaps the most memorable of those sessions was a dinner with Bill Bowen, who had been the president of Princeton and was then the president of the Mellon Foundation. After a long, pleasant dinner and quite a bit of wine, Bill allowed as how he did not know what might make the most sense, but of the organizations that he knew, the one that came closest to the way I described my interest in humanitarian relief and international development was the International Rescue Committee. Since to his knowledge, the IRC was not looking for a new CEO, he suggested that I look for other organizations that seemed similar to it. I had never heard of the International Rescue Committee, but I assured Bill that I would find out more about it and also look for other organizations with a similar purpose.

I proceeded to explore a range of options, including leadership of think tanks and foundations. Then, when I was in my office in the summer of 2001, Jerry Speyer, co-chair of the Columbia board earlier in my tenure, called me to ask what he said he feared was a stupid question: Was there any chance that I could have interest in the International Rescue Committee? I told him the story of my conversation with Bill Bowen and said simply that the answer was Yes. Jerry then said that he had done his part and would hand the phone over to his wife, Katherine Farley, who was the chair of the search committee for a new president of the IRC! Many conversations and interviews later (including with quite a few staff members who were skeptical that an academic who had never been in the development field would be apt for the role), I was offered and accepted the position, with a schedule to start in the summer of 2002.

During our Columbia years, Nancy and I had purchased a get-away place on Pinewood Lake in Trumbull, Connecticut. Nancy had hoped to have a refuge from New York. I recognized that Nancy had not liked the idea of living in New York—indeed, it was the one place in the world that she had said she would not like to live. For someone who grew up on a farm in New Hampshire, it was indeed a very urban environment. I therefore supported her in seeking another location for getting away. But because I liked being in the city and was not eager to get away to just anywhere in the country, I asked that we try to find our second home somewhere on a waterfront—so that we did not leave the city only, as I put it in our discussions, to look out over a neighbor's picket fence.

In 1996, after looking assiduously over several years around every body of water within an hour or a bit more of upper Manhattan, we discovered Pinewood Lake. After watching for several months, we found out about a house in a wonderful setting at the north end of the lake that looked out over a mile of water and was about to go on the market. We bought it right away. We both became very attached to the house, especially after completing significant renovations to open it up more to light and views on its lake side. Stephie and I, with some assists from Kathy and Nancy, built a boat house for our sailboat and canoe that had moved with us from Cambridge to Houston to New York—and also with room over time for a kayak and a wind surfer. The lakefront house was a fine get-away and promised to become a home base.

During their parents' Columbia years, Kathy and Stephie continued to take major steps in their education and relationships.

After their marriage, Kathy and Paolo lived in Chicago for one year. Kathy passed her doctoral general examinations and then received a Japanese Ministry of Education (Mombusho) grant for research in Japan for 1994–96. Paolo completed his post-doctoral research in Chicago and accepted a position as Assistant Professor of Astronomy and Physics at Yale. He and Kathy moved to New Haven in 1994. During the two years that Kathy was conducting her research in Japan, Paolo managed to get grants for Japanese-funded research that allowed him to travel to Japan for brief visits. But they were often apart. Happily Nancy and I also had an opportunity to visit with Kathy while she was doing her fieldwork outside of Tokyo. After Kathy returned to the States, she continued to work on her dissertation with the support first of a National Science Foundation grant and then a special University of Chicago dissertation writing fellowship, and she received her PhD in 1999. Her dissertation was subsequently published in book form by Stanford University Press in 2003 with the title *Gift-Giving in Japan: Cash, Connections, Cosmologies.*

Perhaps most life-changing of all, their first child was born on March 25, 1998: Alexander Marco Rupp-Coppi—with his middle name in honor of a favorite uncle of Paolo who, unlike his parents, continued to live in Italy. For the next years, Kathy would combine caring for her child and then children with full-time academic positions: Lecturer and De Bary Postdoctoral Teaching Fellow in East Asian Civilizations at Columbia's Heyman Center for the Humanities; Postdoctoral Associate at Yale's Council on East Asian Studies. Then, after the birth of their second and third children, Kathy worked part-time in teaching and editing as a Research Affiliate in the Department of Anthropology at Yale. During those years, Paolo continued his research and teaching at Yale in both the departments of astronomy and of physics. He was promoted to associate professor with tenure in 2001 and then to full professor in 2003.

Those years were very eventful for Stephie as well. She completed her MEd degree at Harvard in 1995 and then pursued a PhD in anthropology at Yale, which was awarded in 2001. Her research focused on Africa and included two years of living in southeastern Cameroon, during which she not only acquired further fluency in French but also learned Bangandu, the language of the majority of the residents in the village of fifty or so families where she lived. Nancy and I had the pleasure of visiting her there in December of 1998 and were enormously impressed with how closely integrated she was into the community. In due course, the dissertation based on her time in southeastern Cameroon was published by the University of Washington Press as *Forests of Belonging: Identities, Ethnicities, and Stereotypes in the Congo River Basin* (2011).

Then in December 1999 Stephie, too, had a life-changing event: she and a graduate student whom she had met at Yale, Ju-Hon Kwek, were married in St. Paul's Chapel on the Columbia campus with a grand reception at the Casa Italiana (also on the campus) and a further breakfast gathering at the President's House, followed by further festivities in Singapore, with both sets of parents joining enthusiastically in all the celebrations.

During all of these developments, Nancy's mother and my mother were regularly involved. But their health was also failing. Nancy's mother was increasingly fragile in terms of her mobility and other health concerns. She was living in New Hampshire, and Nancy's brother Charlie and sister Joanne were taking increasing responsibility for overseeing her treatment as she moved from one care center to another. Then just a few months after Stephie's and Ju-Hon's wedding, she died suddenly, though certainly not unexpectedly, in May 2000. She was buried next to Pres in the family plot in Henniker, New Hampshire.

Some years earlier, in 1994, my mother decided that she would like to move from the retirement community where she had lived since my father's death more than twenty years earlier to a progressive care facility so that she would be certain not to become a burden on any of her family. She was thinking of a progressive care place near where she was then living in New Jersey because she knew a few others who had moved there and liked it. But then Kathy and Paolo moved to New Haven. As she and I talked about options, we agreed that if she could find a similar facility in Connecticut, the whole family would be more able to see each other regularly. We did indeed find a similar and even better facility in North Branford, Connecticut—to which my mother moved in 1994 just as Kathy and Paolo were about to move to New Haven, and where she lived until she died in 2012, at the age of ninety-five.

Fourth Quarter

Global Stretch

(2002-)

FOR NANCY AND ME, the fourth quarter began with Pinewood Lake and Trumbull as home base. Nancy became increasingly involved with the community and in particular with its libraries. She was invited to join the board of the longest established library in Trumbull—in the historic center of the village of Nichols, which over time was merged into Trumbull. This small very much local resource was called the Fairchild Nichols Library because it was one of the libraries that the Fairchilds endowed. Nancy continues to enjoy service on this board with fellow members who have become good friends. She was also elected to the board for the larger Trumbull Library, which is a much more politicized body because its board members receive approval from elected town authorities.

Along with her library duties, Nancy's biggest involvement besides her family is the First Presbyterian Church in New Haven. Both Nancy and I became very close to Maria LaSalla and Bill Goettler, the co-pastors when we first started attending. Nancy was active in the Mission Committee, which took responsibility for community outreach locally and globally. She especially enjoyed getting the church involved with and supportive of Bread for the World. Before long she became co-chair of the Mission Committee and then was also elected to serve two terms as an Elder, which means membership in the Session (the ruling body of the local church).

For Kathy as well, the years following the family move from Chicago to New Haven were eventful. Along with her appointments as lecturer and teaching fellow at Columbia and post-doctoral associate and research affiliate at Yale, Kathy became engaged with a wide range of community responsibilities, which increased as their family grew. Living initially in a Yale residential college as residential advisors and following that in an apartment in central New Haven, the Rupp-Coppi family then moved to an apartment in Woodbridge on the western outskirts of the city. But when they decided to purchase their own home, they focused on the educational quality of local schools. Based on that criterion, they decided to settle in Madison, Connecticut—an outlying suburb to the east of New Haven along the coast.

The family continued to grow. While Kathy, Paolo, and Alex were still living in Woodbridge, on May 13, 2002, Leo Farrar Rupp-Coppi was born—with a middle name that honored his maternal grandmother's family. Then after the move to Madison, on May 19, 2004, Erika Marie Rupp-Coppi was born—named after her maternal great grandmother Erika and her paternal grandmother Maria (though with a change in the final vowel that her father thought flowed better because it would not entail two ending "a" sounds in her first and middle names). Erika was born in Colorado on the first step of the family's sabbatical year that included time in at the University of Colorado, the University of Heidelberg, and Stanford.

Kathy continued to be involved in academics at Yale, but she also expanded her community service work. For example, she co-chaired a book fair for Madison schools, she was a classroom co-ordinator who organized projects for students and other volunteer activities, and she was the co-chair of the Madison civics committee that was responsible for food drives, senior citizen programs, and Habitat for Humanity work in New Haven. Perhaps most time and energy consuming, she became the coach for the Madison public schools Odyssey of the Mind program, in which four of the six teams she coached placed first or second in Connecticut state finals and then went on to the world finals in Maryland, Iowa, and Michigan, where they placed in the top ten. In and around all of these academic and civic engagements, Kathy also joined a writing group in which members read and discussed each other's current projects—in her case a novel she wrote that is based in Japan and is rich in cross-cultural texture (including crucial scenes in a Buddhist monastery).

For Stephie, too, these years were very eventful. The week following their wedding, she and Ju-Hon moved to Singapore, where he had to complete his national service and then worked as a senior administrator in the defense department. Stephie got a faculty appointment in the National University of Singapore, starting in 2001. She thoroughly enjoyed her teaching, especially on Africa, about which it is fair to note she knew a lot more than others in Singapore. She received the NUS Teaching Excellence Award multiple times, along with special incentive grants for outstanding teaching. She taught not only in the sociology department but was also in the University Scholars Programme, which was an honors program. She also served for a year as assistant dean with responsibility for the University Scholars Programme.

Stephie and Ju-Hon first purchased an apartment in a leafy green neighborhood near the university. But they then also embarked on an ambitious restoration project when they purchased a historical Chinese shop house, full of ornate temple carvings lining the interior, and renovated it into a spacious residence.

Children followed: Kai-Lin Kwek-Rupp, born on March 29, 2004, and Kai-Shan Kwek-Rupp, born on March 14, 2006. As is a frequent custom in Chinese families, male siblings and paternal cousins share a character to denote their generation. Stephie and Ju-Hon decided to have their children, whether boys or girls, share a common first syllable: "Kai." For the girl or girls, the "Kai" would be the pronunciation of the character for "joyful." For the boy or boys, the "Kai" would be the pronunciation of the character for "victorious." In the end, the children of Ju-Hon's brothers—the cousins of Stephie's and Ju-Hon's children—were also given names starting with "Kai" and sharing the same characters, preserving the Chinese naming tradition.

Even as Kai-Shan was coming into the world, his parents decided that they would be moving back to the United States at least for a while. Ju-Hon had concluded that he would like to broaden his working horizons by earning an MBA. He applied and was admitted to Harvard Business School. Meanwhile, Stephie secured appointments as a faculty associate in the Intrastate Conflict Program at the Kennedy School of Government and as a research fellow at the International Security Program, also at the Kennedy School. The result was two very full years of caring for children and engaging in demanding study and research and then also applying for positions for the following years.

For me, too, the years following 2002 were enormously engaging. Indeed, as much as I relished each of my previous positions, serving as president of the International Rescue Committee was my favorite assignment. I loved the mission of the IRC, I valued my committed colleagues and gained great satisfaction from working with them to make a great organization even better, and I especially enjoyed visiting programs in the field across this country and around the world.

There were also stresses in my role at the IRC, beginning with a quite arduous commute. In my past positions, I had at most a few miles between home and work—two miles in Redlands, which I often biked, or three miles in Green Bay. Indeed, for most of my previous positions, I walked to work: across the street at Harvard, a hundred yards or so on campus at Rice, two blocks at Columbia. For the IRC, it was at a minimum an hour and forty-five minutes each way: twenty minutes by car to the station, an hour and twenty minutes on the express train, and then a short walk across 42nd Street from Grand Central Terminal to the IRC headquarters at the corner of 42nd Street and Lexington Avenue. Nancy and I had agreed that we would see whether the commuting was feasible as a long-term arrangement. If not, we agreed we would get an apartment in the city as a second place.

But it turned out that I rather liked the time on the train. Instead of less than five minutes between work and home, I had more time as a break. I used that time for reading and reflection—not for email or for continuing work (which I would take up again upon arrival at home). My schedule meant leaving home a little before 6 a.m. and arriving back home at about 7:45 p.m. if all went well. That schedule in turn meant that I could be at the office by 7:45 a.m. and stay until a little after 6 p.m.—which allowed me to set an example of serious work time for my colleagues in the office. That was my daily schedule except when I was somewhere else in the country or the world (which admittedly was quite often) or when I had an evening event in New York (also not infrequent), in which case I would stay in a hotel near the IRC for the night.

I enjoyed my colleagues at the IRC enormously. My predecessor, Reynold Levy, had recruited excellent senior colleagues. While I retained most of the core team, I did make a few changes. One such change was in the chief financial officer. After reaching agreement that the existing CFO would move on, I recruited Pat Long for this role. I knew her from Columbia, which she had left to become the CFO for Save the Children—a perfect background to become the outstanding colleague that she was at the IRC.

In each of my positions, I was convinced that the way to build an institution was to make it more itself rather than to have it imitate some other organization. At the IRC there was a major challenge in this regard. When I arrived, my predecessor advised me to avoid the term "development" in talking about the mission of the IRC, even though it was increasingly involved in international development work. The reason behind this advice was straightforward: a core of the board felt strongly that the IRC should focus on its original mandate of rescuing refugees and resettling them in the United States—the mandate that had guided the organization since it was founded in 1933 at the suggestion of Albert Einstein that there be a committee of notables in New York to work with counterparts in Europe to rescue refugees from the Nazis and help them to become resettled in America. International involvement should therefore be restricted to emergency interventions intended to rescue displaced people for resettlement.

Upon examining the actual work of the IRC, I concluded that development was not only an important part of its activities but that it was becoming an ever greater part. The reason was straightforward: as there were more and more displaced people in the world, only a very small proportion of them could qualify for resettlement in the U.S. or other developed countries. The vast majority would have to be integrated into the countries to which they had fled or be reintegrated into their home countries if and when they returned.

At the same time, I concluded that the work the IRC was doing internationally was not at all inconsistent with its founding mandate. The trajectory from refugee to resettlement had as its counterpart the movement from being uprooted to being supported in re-establishing life either in the country of refuge or back home—which in both cases required the basic economic development that the IRC worked to provide through emergency relief, health care, education, and livelihood training. In my first year at the IRC, even those most dedicated to the core mission of the organization tracing back to Einstein came to agree that this understanding of development as the international counterpart of resettlement in the U.S. was consistent with the mandate of the organization. In the coming years this overall mandate was captured in the tagline "From Harm to Home."

Reynold Levy was a very enthusiastic and effective fundraiser, which he demonstrated at the 92nd Street Y (before coming to the IRC) and at Lincoln Center (after leaving the IRC). At the IRC, he was the driving force in launching a sixty-million-dollar capital campaign. He had engaged a consultant, Janet Harris, to conduct a feasibility study for a campaign of this scale at the IRC. Her report made it clear that she thought the IRC was not yet ready for such an effort. Reynold's response was classic: to hire her as vice president for development, with the understanding that a campaign would indeed go forward, with her leading the effort at the staff level!

The campaign had achieved substantial success—one could argue, by plucking the low-hanging fruit of board members and long-term supporters. But by the time Reynold announced his decision to move on (the initial plan was that he would teach about non-profits at Harvard Business School, but he was then offered and accepted the position of president of Lincoln Center), the IRC campaign had lost some of its momentum after raising a bit over thirty million dollars. My task was to re-energize the campaign so that it could include many new donors, a task in which I was very fortunate to have Janet Harris as a dedicated and imaginative colleague. In a handful of years, the campaign was indeed re-energized and surpassed its initial goal of sixty million dollars. We then increased the goal to one hundred million dollars, and we ended the campaign with a declaration of victory in 2011, having raised just over one hundred ten million dollars.

Raising private money for the new endowment and also for ongoing programs was an important priority for the IRC. Private sources were crucial because they were the main source of unrestricted moneys that could be invested wherever the need was greatest. But in the end only about 15% of the annual budget came from private sources. I was concerned that a very high proportion of the other 85% of annual income came from the U.S. government. I determined early on that this part of the IRC revenue stream needed to be diversified, and I made that a further priority. By the end of my time as president, the budget of the IRC had more than tripled—from one hundred thirty million dollars to four hundred fifty million dollars. Even though much more money was being raised, the ratio of private to public funds remained almost exactly the same—15% private and 85% public. But of the 85% that was public, the part that came from countries or agencies other than the U.S. government was much larger—indeed more than half. The result was that the IRC was a significantly more international organization, which meant that it could intervene internationally in ways that it deemed required whether or not those interventions represented a priority of the U.S. government.

In my first year at the IRC, I addressed as well what I thought was another institutional priority: the governance of the organization. The IRC had a very impressive board that included some very active members. But the board was simply too large to serve as a fiduciary for the organization, since it had some eighty-five members. This large board included many well-known and influential and helpful members—for example, Elie Wiesel, Henry Kissinger, Liv Ullmann, Robin Chandler Duke, Princess Firyal of Jordan, Michael Blumenthal, and Andy Grove.

Andy Grove, the founder of Intel, is arresting example of why rethinking the board structure was imperative. When I first met with him in California in fall of my first year, Andy—whom the IRC had resettled as a refugee from Hungary and who was a generous donor—was very thoughtful and supportive, but he said that he felt he had to resign from the board, since he rarely attended meetings and could not claim to exercise any fiduciary responsibility for the organization. I responded that he should wait a few months before taking that step because I was sure that he would be open to a new alternative that would be better than simply resigning.

The board had an executive committee of about thirty members, most of whom attended meetings regularly and also participated in committees. I consulted carefully with key board members and elicited agreement to restructure the board so that most of the executive committee members would constitute the board, while a new entity—to be called the IRC Overseers (a shameless appropriation of the well-known Harvard term for its large advisory board that had very few formal governance responsibilities)—would provide advice and serve as advocates and fundraisers and other outwardly facing services. After many hours of consultation and deliberation, this restructuring was implemented without losing the participation of a single one of the eighty-five members, since some fifty-five were happy to be the first Overseers. Andy Grove, for example, was pleased to be an Overseer, though he was ready to resign from the board. Furthermore, the role of the Overseers as advocates and advisors allowed the IRC to recruit new members who would not join if they were to be full board members who had to attend meetings and exercise fiduciary responsibilities. As a result, the IRC in short order added Madeline Albright, Colin Powell, Jim Wolfensohn, and Kofi Annan as Overseers.

In sum, from the beginning of my time as president, I energetically pursued these crucial administrative goals: shaping the identity of the IRC to include development as the international counterpart of resettlement and therefore integral to the core agenda of the organization; fundraising to achieve raised goals for both current use gifts and the endowment; a rebalancing of the government funding portfolio to be significantly less dependent on the U.S.; and restructuring the institutional governance of the institution.

But I also was enormously impressed by and drawn to the programs that the IRC implemented on the ground. Consequently, I made it a priority to visit both resettlement offices in the U.S. and country programs abroad. Over the years, I visited all twenty-two resettlement offices and virtually all of the international offices and programs. Included were six trips each to Afghanistan (including one after the tragic killing of four IRC staff members) and Sudan (including South Sudan, Darfur, and Sudan), five to the Democratic Republic of Congo, several each to Pakistan, Indonesia, Liberia, Sierra Leone, Burundi, Kenya, Uganda, Rwanda, Thailand, Iraq, Turkey, Syria, and Myanmar, and quite a few other quick one-time visits—for example to Mali and the Central African Republic.

As I frequently noted, when I was the dean of Harvard Divinity School and the president of Rice and Columbia, I traveled across the country and around the world to centers of high culture where prominent alumni/ae and supporters lived to ask for their contributions and thank them for their support. At the IRC I had the opportunity as well to visit all of the other intriguing places in the world—not as a tourist or a fundraiser but as a colleague who was very warmly welcomed by fellow IRC staff delighted to host me and those traveling with me (quite often including Nancy) to see their important work. It is tempting to tell endless stories. But describing one resettlement office and one international program will have to suffice.

The resettlement office is the one in Salt Lake City, Utah. It has a full suite of programs like those in the other large IRC resettlement centers. Staff and volunteers secure an apartment, provide furnishings, and purchase food and other essentials for initial settling into a new home. They then welcome the refugees (usually a family) at an arrival point (usually the nearest airport). After helping with the moving-in process, staff and volunteers work closely with the new arrivals to find work for the adults and schooling for any children. In executing these tasks, long-term involvement is a major asset. For example, the IRC typically has an array of prospective employers who have been very impressed with the diligence and work habits of refugees resettled in the past and therefore are eager for new recruits. Similarly, there is accumulated experience to help children in adjusting to new schools, including tutoring by wonderful volunteers. In all of these respects, the Salt Lake City office is typical.

But it is unusual in one respect. In rare cases, resettlement does not go well in the initial placement. In those unusual instances, the IRC employs what it terms "secondary placement." Before I visited, I was aware of the fact that the Salt Lake City office was very often the preferred site selected for such second tries. It puzzled me that such a conservative area of the country would be chosen for this task. The mystery was quickly solved at least in my mind once I visited. Salt Lake City is unusually hospitable because it is populated with so many members of the Church of the Latter Day Saints (actually, the Mormon population of Salt Lake City is lower than that of Utah as a whole, but it is still about 45%). Many Mormons, especially males, serve abroad as missionaries in their late teens or early twenties. As a result, Salt Lake City is like a place in which about half of the population are returned overseas volunteers themselves, and many more are in families with members who have lived for extended periods in overseas locations. They know what it is like to be outsiders in a new country, to learn new languages and ways of living; and they identify with the challenges that need to be addressed for refugee families in analogous situations in the United States. Many of these Mormons in Utah become volunteers with the IRC, and in any case they establish an ethos for the city that is unusually welcoming.

Just as I have resisted the temptation to discuss all of the IRC's resettlement programs, I will also focus on one of the many countries in which it has international programs. Overall, the international programs are much more extensive than the IRC's domestic operations. In financial terms, they account for over 80% of the program expenses. They are also very dynamic in that they are usually triggered by a conflict or other emergency. But then they also carry on for years, even decades.

Of the dozens of countries in which the IRC operates outside the U.S., it has the longest presence in Afghanistan, which is in any case among the most fascinating of the international settings. The IRC has been involved with Afghan refugees in Pakistan since 1980, when they fled following the invasion by the Soviet Union in 1979. The long-term work with Afghan refugees in Pakistan was crucial for educating a generation of Afghans to take responsibility for their country in the future. The IRC established its presence in Afghanistan itself in 1988 as the Soviet forces withdrew. It quickly established local schools and continued to operate them all even during the rule of the Taliban. The schools educated girls as well as boys—which the Taliban grudgingly allowed because parents insisted that their daughters as well as their sons should be educated.

By the time I visited Afghanistan the first time in 2002, the Taliban government had been overthrown, and a transitional government outlined in the so-called Bonn Agreement was in place. Because this trip was with a delegation of board members—three of whom were former U.S. ambassadors—the State Department insisted that the delegation travel with armed guards from the Afghan army as escorts in front of and behind our three car convoy. If this trip had not been among my first for the IRC and also my first to Afghanistan, I would have refused the armed escorts because they drew unneeded attention to the IRC and threatened to identify IRC offices and residences as future targets. I felt less safe than on any of my other trips, even though on those other trips I travelled in much less secure areas. The difference was that on the other trips I was traveling quietly with Afghan staff, who knew the areas and were known there.

This difference is also the reason why I was regularly invited to stop by the U.S. Embassy in Kabul after my trips to visit IRC programs. I readily agreed to what I first thought would just be a courtesy call. But as senior American personnel, including a series of ambassadors, engaged in extended conversations, it became clear that they were extremely interested in learning about regions that they were not allowed to visit—or could visit only with elaborate security details. The contrast in security also explains why the IRC consistently refused to accept funding that came from the U.S. government through what were termed Provincial Reconstruction Teams, which were supposed to be whole-of-government teams and often disbursed funding from the civilian side of the U.S. but were in fact controlled by the military leadership.

I relished my trips to Afghanistan because it was an opportunity to see the long-term impact of the IRC in a developing country. Local staff would proudly point out apple orchards filled with ripening fruit and note that the trees were planted soon after the IRC began its work in Afghanistan. Similarly, I would be shown irrigation systems or small rural hospitals that the IRC had helped to build over the decades of its presence. Or staff would talk about their education in IRC-founded schools. Indeed, when I and a small delegation of IRC colleagues met with Afghanistan's first elected president, Hamid Karzai, he proudly recounted his experience as a teacher of English in the IRC school for Afghan refugees in Peshawar, Pakistan.

Perhaps the program that best captures the IRC's efforts in Afghanistan is the National Solidarity Program, which was initially funded by the World Bank. The IRC was very much involved in designing the program in multiple ways. For starters, the former deputy director of IRC programs in Afghanistan, Haneef Atmar, became the Minister of Rural Development in the Karzai government. Through his involvement with the IRC, Haneef knew that

Rwanda had faced issues similar to those confronting Afghanistan in that it, too, had a central government concentrated in its capital that needed to find ways to connect with villages all across its admittedly much smaller total area. With the eager cooperation of colleagues in the IRC, Haneef organized a workshop in which a delegation from IRC-Rwanda travelled to Kabul to report on their experience and thereby advise how a similar program might be established in Afghanistan. The result in time was the National Solidarity Program.

It was a community development initiative implemented by Afghan staff in which the first step was to form (usually by election) a village council that would listen to all constituencies as to what were the highest development priorities. Almost always that meant a health clinic or a school or a water system. With some outside funding for supplies and, if needed, professional advice, the projects would be undertaken through the work of villagers, who would be compensated if they were as a result of their commitment to the project unable to maintain their work to provide for their basic livelihoods, and if the village council approved. Over time the IRC was involved in this effort in over three thousand villages. Some of my most exhilarating moments in Afghanistan were visiting these projects, including ones in which the remarkable craftsmanship of local laborers was evident in gorgeous stone work for the buildings or bridges or overpasses that were constructed. Because of the success of the initial World Bank-funded program, other governments (including the U.S.) and foundations as well provided funding, and other NGOs also implemented similar programs. The result was that the National Solidarity Program was implemented in over thirty thousand villages across Afghanistan.

I loved all of my work over the decades, but my years at the IRC were my favorite time. It was a wonderful experience. My colleagues on the staff were terrific. The board and loyal donors—both the exemplary (indeed famous) members who came to comprise the core of the Overseers and also the hard-working regular board members—were great. The identity of the organization, captured in the new tag-line "From Harm to Home," was deeply compelling.

Yet the time for a transition was coming. My rule of thumb for the appropriate length of time to serve as the leader of any institution is ten years give or take two. That rule of thumb provided enough time to make a meaningful and lasting contribution, while not remaining in a leadership position for so long that the institution lost momentum and creative energy. Also, in 2012 I would turn seventy.

The IRC had a lot of momentum under way: the budget that had more than tripled was continuing its growth, both public and private fundraising had achieved records (including the $110 one hundred-ten-million-dollar capital campaign), the profile of the IRC was higher than it had been (thanks in significant part to a "re-branding" program deeply indebted to the work of Christoph Becker, board member, frequent fellow traveler to field sites, and devoted pro-bono contributor of his expertise in advertising and public relations), morale was high across the now over 12,000 staff (with 98% of the IRC staff in programs abroad working in and contributing to their home countries), and a very able senior team was in place. The time to recruit an outstanding successor was at hand.

In the spring of 2012 I informed my colleagues on the staff and the board of my intention to step down in the following summer. In due course a search committee was formed and the position was posted. There was a lot of interest both from within the IRC and from outsiders. In the end, despite the attractiveness of several inside candidates, the search committee was unanimous in choosing David Miliband, the former foreign secretary and leader of the Labor Party in the UK. I was consulted at every stage of the search process and was also engaged in persuading David to accept the position. He came with the charge of maintaining the momentum under way at the IRC and in particular of continuing to raise its profile as a leading NGO in international relief and development and resettlement, and he has fulfilled and continues to fulfill that mandate admirably.

During my very active years at the IRC, Kathy too remained very engaged. At the center of her involvements was raising the three Rupp-Coppi children. Along with caring for them and investing in the very considerable community activities that entailed, she continued her academic work at Yale and engaged in tutoring, advising, and editing, in particular with international students. Through her work as classroom coordinator in the local elementary school and her coaching of Madison's Odyssey of the Mind program, she became interested in teaching at the secondary level and undertook an intensive teaching accreditation program for which she had to travel to Hartford for classes and to gain teaching experience. There followed three positions in pretty quick succession: full-time teacher of modern Western culture at the Hebrew Academy, an orthodox Jewish school on the western end of New Haven; researcher and writer for Pericles Lewis, president of the Yale-NUS College in Singapore, and a senior member of the New Haven staff that provided support for the college; and research and fundraising associate for the Yale central development office, her current position.

In addition to caring for Alexander, Leo, and Erika, Kathy played a further crucial role for the family in providing companionship and support for my mother Erika. The Rupp-Coppi home was only about fifteen minutes from the continuous care facility where my mother lived in Branford. I visited her every weekend when I was not somewhere else in the world. But Kathy made a point of visiting with her on multiple occasions each week. It was in a way like going back to her college days: when she was a student at Princeton, Kathy and my mother both lived in southern New Jersey and could spend time together when most of the rest of the family was far away in Texas. Toward the end of my mother's life until she died in 2012, Kathy was an invaluable source of loving care for her.

Stephie as well was very active during these years. After Ju-Hon completed his MBA, he accepted a position at McKinsey as a full-time consultant, with a focus on finance, especially in its international dimension. He was to be based in New York City. Stephie therefore explored positions either in New York or within a reasonable commuting distance. In the end she decided to accept a position as Assistant Professor of Anthropology at Lehman College, which is part of the City University of New York. The family moved to New York in the summer of 2008 and lived on the Upper West Side, first in a tiny one-bedroom apartment overlooking the Hudson River, then on 79th Street and Amsterdam, where the family finally had two bedrooms in a compact apartment, and then on 108th Street and Broadway, where they purchased a co-op with considerably more space.

At Lehman College, Stephie taught four courses every fall semester and three courses every spring semester, with the supervision of innumerable student research projects in addition. As Kai-Lin and Kai-Shan grew up, she also coached multiple soccer teams on the Upper West Side. At the same time, she saw the revised version of her dissertation through to publication, edited two further books, and wrote a number of articles and book chapters. Both Stephie and Ju-Hon were extremely busy with their demanding jobs and their two children.

But then a further major variable was introduced into their lives. Kathy's first two children were both boys, and because she very much hoped to have a daughter, she became pregnant again—and Erika was born. Stephie had a boy and a girl and was incredibly busy. Nancy and I kind of assumed that there would be no further grandchildren. Stephie and Ju-Hon decided that they would have a third child. Appropriately for their new location, Kai-Jin Kwek-Rupp was born on March 8 (an auspicious day according to Chinese tradition), 2010, in a New York taxi on the way to the hospital, as Nancy and I were also on the way from Trumbull to take care of Kai-Lin and Kai-Shan, which a neighbor covered until we could arrive!

In addition to the birth of Kai-Jin, Stephie and Ju-Hon had a further wonderful development a few years after his birth. Within months of each other in 2014, Ju-Hon became a partner at McKinsey, and Stephie received tenure and was promoted to Associate Professor at Lehman College. Their family was in solid financial shape and at least for the foreseeable future firmly anchored in New York City.

Nancy, too, was very busy during these years. She was always available to help with the grandchildren—as was I, though at a lesser level of availability and competence. She also continued to be the networker who kept in touch with family and friends. Three examples illustrate that role as persistent connector. (I have already mentioned the first two examples in that they were also relevant at earlier points in our joint narrative, but I ask for indulgence of the repetition and expansion into our fourth quarter because they exemplify the overall pattern of Nancy's social interactions so well.)

First, Nancy has over the years kept in close contact with four couples with whom she and I have met regularly for the more than fifty years since the ten of us first met in and around Boston. The meetings have included frequent visits and wonderful trips, for example, canoeing down the Allagash River in Maine. Often all ten participate, but on more than one occasion the five women have taken off on a trip by themselves when the men were either not interested or unavailable—for example to Big Bend National Park, which Nancy has come to know and love since living in Texas.

Second, Nancy has participated in a book group since the early days of residence in New York City. She attended while living in the city, but she has continued to travel in to attend meetings during the years that Nancy and I have lived full-time in Trumbull. This book group celebrated its fortieth anniversary in 2018: it started fifteen years before Nancy joined, but she has been a faithful member for twenty-five years.

Third, Nancy organized a quite elaborate celebration for our fiftieth wedding anniversary, a large gathering that included extended family members and friends from over the decades.

As for me, many of my activities have continued after I "retired" from the IRC. I am still connected to the IRC as an Overseer and offer advice and counsel whenever asked for it. During my time at the IRC, I served on the board of InterAction (a coalition of NGOs) and also on the board of the U.S. Global Leadership Coalition (with one term as co-chair), but those positions were based in significant part on my presidency of the IRC and therefore ended with my time as CEO. I continue to be a board member of the Institute for International Education and its Scholar Rescue Committee and also of the Henry Luce Foundation (and served in 2019 as the chair of the search committee that found a new president). But I have reached the term limit for my service on the Josiah Macy Foundation board, and I declined to be re-elected to the board of the American Academy in Berlin. A major new assignment has been to be chair of the International Baccalaureate Organization, a remarkable institution that implements and then oversees programs in over five thousand schools around the world and has an international board that meets at the IB's various global centers: Geneva; the Hague; Bethesda, Maryland; and Singapore.

For the two years right after I completed my time at the IRC, through the generosity of the Carnegie Corporation, I held an appointment as Senior Fellow at the Carnegie Council for Ethics in International Affairs, a position that allowed me to focus on the book that was published in 2015 as *Beyond Individualism: The Challenge of Inclusive Communities*. It is a book that illustrates the change that had occurred in my writing over the decades. While my first three books were clearly academic works based on my study and research during my time as a graduate student and faculty member, this book and its two predecessors are revised and at times expanded versions of talks or papers that I wrote over a period of years while most of my time and energy was focused on leading institutions. In the case of *Commitment and Community*, the core material was from lectures and essays written during my time as dean of Harvard Divinity School (even though the book was not published until 1989, with the encouragement of Michael West, an HDS colleague who then went into publishing). *Globalization Challenged: Conviction, Conflict, Community*, based on the Schoff Lectures at Columbia in 2003 and published in 2006, drew on materials from my first year at the IRC and included responses to the lectures from colleagues at Columbia. *Beyond Individualism* develops some of the same themes further even as the argument connects to themes also evident in my earliest work. Especially during the years at the IRC, I also moved from more academic articles to advocacy pieces and opinion essays (op-eds), frequently issued with multiple co-authors.

While I was at the Carnegie Council, two good friends and colleagues for five decades—Wayne Proudfoot and Mark Taylor—pressed me to consider teaching one course each semester in the religion department at Columbia. I agreed and decided to teach two courses that would alternate: Religion and International Development—Theory and Practice; and Religion and Modern Western Individualism. I thoroughly enjoyed the interaction with students from all over the university that the seminar format allowed. Yet as much as I found the teaching stimulating and liked discussions with my colleagues on the faculty, I reluctantly came to the conclusion that I would not continue the teaching after the third semester. My role with the International Baccalaureate became quite demanding and time-consuming, including considerable international travel, which made being on campus every week at the appointed time complicated. But perhaps more fundamentally, I was increasingly uncomfortable with being one more senior white male in a department with four other men in their seventies.

I participated in a further new initiative upon completing my time at the IRC. I joined with a few colleagues from over the years—Alberta Arthurs, Vishahka Desai, Jonathan Fanton, and Regina Peruggi—to establish a consulting organization, which we named NEXT, Transition Advisors. It was devoted to assisting not-for-profit organizations in negotiating transitions of all sorts but especially in leadership. It continues to implement this mission. But I have stepped away from my role in this consultancy, as my participation confirmed my sense that my efforts are most effective and impactful when I am an organizer or an executive rather than an advisor or a consultant.

I have continued to give lectures and talks and presentations for special occasions in these "retirement" years. For example, I was the Distinguished Visiting Scarff Professor at Lawrence University in Wisconsin in the fall of 2016. I also addressed the Salisbury Forum in Connecticut and was the inaugural keynote speaker for the Harvard Divinity School Centennial Celebration, both also in the fall of 2016. Examples of participation in the observation of special occasions include speaking at the symposium to celebrate the contributions of Jim Laney to Emory University and multiple occasions at Rice: the twenty-fifth anniversary of the Keck Center for the Biological Sciences—ongoing funding for which I was instrumental in securing; the twentieth anniversary of the DeLange multidisciplinary conferences; speaker at the Rice Commencement; the Centennial of Rice; and more soberly, the memorial service for good friend and Rice supporter Demaris Hudspeth (when both Nancy and I spoke), and the funeral and burial of our close friend and colleague Ralph O'Connor (for whom I was an honorary pallbearer).

Challenges continue for all. Kathy and Stephie focus enormous energy in supporting their families and especially in raising their children. Alex is completing his sophomore year at Columbia; Leo spent his junior year of high school in Italy, is now completing his senior year in the Madison school system, and has decided that Princeton is the university where he will go for his undergraduate education; and Erika is completing her sophomore year of high school. Kai-Lin and Kai-Shan are engaging the complicated public and private school choices in New York City as they move from middle to high school, and Kai-Jin will soon follow. All three of the Kwek-Rupp kids have travelled with their mother to visit southeastern Cameroon in 2018 and 2019, staying in the village in which Stephie has lived for several years on and off over the past quarter century. Stephie is, as usual, far too busy but seems able to juggle her immense load. Kathy continues to look for the optimal professional trajectory for the years ahead.

Meanwhile Nancy and I are getting used to being more or less retired. We are not yet at the close of our fourth quarter. But as for all of us, that endpoint is getting nearer.

Index

(pages in **bold** indicate photos)

Index

Index

Index

Index

Index

87